# Let's Get Out of Japan!

### 英語で世界に橋を架けよう
〜海外で学ぶ・働く・異文化を知るための総合英語〜

川村義治／Gavin Lynch

NAN'UN-DO

Let's Get Out of Japan!

Copyright © 2015

by

Yoshiharu Kawamura

Gavin Lynch

All Rights Reserved.

No part of this book may be reproduced in any form without written permission from the authors and Nan'un-do Co., Ltd.

このテキストの音声を無料で視聴（ストリーミング）・ダウンロードできます。自習用音声としてご活用ください。
以下のサイトにアクセスしてテキスト番号で検索してください。

**https://nanun-do.com**　テキスト番号 [ **511687** ]

※ 無線 LAN（WiFi）に接続してのご利用を推奨いたします。

※ 音声ダウンロードは Zip ファイルでの提供になります。
　お使いの機器によっては別途ソフトウェア（アプリケーション）の導入が必要となります。

Let's Get Out of Japan! 音声ダウンロードページは左記の QR コードからもご利用になれます。

## はじめに

　本書は、留学、インターンシップ、ボランティアといった明確な活動意識を持って海外に出かける架空の若者の姿を通じて、英語力の向上と異文化理解の促進を目的とする英語学習教材です。同じ大学に通う大学生たちが国際交流センターを通じて世界各地に旅立つというストーリーで、著者たちの経験、書籍から得た知識、報道等からの情報に基づいて書き下ろしています。本書を使用する大学生のみなさんが、英語を学びつつ、留学やインターンシップの手続き、留学先での学習、現地でのホームステイや寮生活、各国の社会状況に関して理解を深められるように、内容や質問を次のような方針と構成により作成しています。

## 作成方針

　本書の内容は次のような方針に基づいています。

### 1　海外で役立つ表現と知識
　学習者が実際に海外で学ぶ際に役立つと思われる英語表現や知識を教材としてできるだけ取り入れるようにしています。

### 2　設定人物とともに経験を深めるストーリー展開
　虚構の中でこそ人は自由に思考を働かすことができるという考えのもと、本書を読み進めるにつれて学習者が登場人物とともに英語力を上げ、海外留学や世界各地の事情を深く理解できるように話の展開を工夫しています。

### 3　各設問内容の関連づけ
　リーディング、リスニング、語彙・文法、ライティングの各領域で扱う意味内容は、できるだけ各章の話題に関連づけて学習の効率化をはかっています。

### 4　地域の実情に合った英語表記
　英語のスペルや表記の仕方は、地域によって幾分異なることがあります。例えば、Mr. Johnson は英国式ではピリオドを省いてしばしば Mr Johnson と書きます。本書でも表記はその地域の実情を考慮しています。

## 内容構成

　本書は 15 章から成り、入門編：留学した学生からの報告（6章分）、発展編：新たな留学希望者との対話（5章分）、冒険編：新たな出会いを求めて（4章分）の3つパートで構成されています。各章はさらに次のように組み立てられています。

### 🌐 I. Vocabulary Preview

　主にリーディングの箇所から6つの基本語彙が選ばれています。日本語の意味を確認してください。

### 🌐 II. Introduction

　次のリーディングの内容紹介です。CD の音声に合わせてさっと読み、これからのストーリー展開を頭に描きましょう。

### 🌐 III. Reading

　海外に出かけた学生からのメール、あるいは学生と別な人物との対話という形式で書かれた内容で、約250語前後の英文です。語句の用法、文法事項、そして内容把握に関する確認問題を含みます。
　尚、フォーマットにつきましては、学習面に配慮し、見易さを重視しております。

### 🌐 IV. Listening

　対話を聴いて情報を把握する学習と対話の一部を読んで内容理解をすすめる学習を行います。

### 🌐 V. Collocations

　英語学習で必要とされる基本的な連語を各章のストーリーを生かした背景のもとで学びます。

### 🌐 VI. Writing

　登場人物のブログの一部を英訳するという形式の英作文です。例示された日本文と英文にならって、また選択肢を考慮に入れながら作業をすすめます。

　本書が留学に関心のある学生、英語の基本的な用法を身に付けたいと思っている学生に意欲を持って英語を学ぶ機会を提供できることを願っています。
　最後に、本書の構想の段階から出版に至るまで南雲堂の丸小雅臣氏に大変お世話になりました。心から感謝の意を表します。

著者一同

# 目　次

**Part Ⅰ　入門編：**
留学している学生からの報告

**Part Ⅱ　発展編：**
新たな留学希望者との対話

**Part Ⅲ　冒険編：**
新たな出会いを求めて

はじめに ─────────────── Ⅲ

**Chapter 1**　*Home Stay in Canada (Yumi)*
カナダの語学留学（バンクーバー）　6

**Chapter 2**　*Home Stay in Australia (Masaru)*
オーストラリアの語学留学（パース）　12

**Chapter 3**　*Home Stay in Britain (Kenta)*
イギリスの語学留学（エジンバラ）　18

**Chapter 4**　*Internship in Singapore (Miki)*
シンガポールのインターンシップ体験（シンガポール）　24

**Chapter 5**　*Home Stay in Ireland (Maria)*
アイルランドの語学留学（ダブリン）　30

**Chapter 6**　*Internship Program in the USA (Kazu)*
アメリカ合衆国のインターンシップ体験（ワシントン D.C.）　36

**Review Test Ⅰ**　　Chapter 1 － Chapter 6
コロケーション　42

**Chapter 7**　*Questions about Canada (from Atsushi to Yumi)*
カナダの語学留学（バンクーバー）　44

**Chapter 8**　*Questions about Australia (from Mariko to Masaru)*
オーストラリアの語学留学（パース）　50

**Chapter 9**　*Questions about Britain (from Naomi to Kenta)*
イギリスの寮生活（エジンバラ）　56

**Chapter 10**　*Questions about Singapore (from Satoko to Miki)*
シンガポールのインターンシップ（シンガポール）　62

**Chapter 11**　*Questions about Ireland (from Shinichi to Maria)*
アイルランドの観光（ダブリン）　68

**Review Test Ⅱ**　　Chapter 7 － Chapter 11
コロケーション　74

**Chapter 12**　*Applying for an Internship Program in Washington D.C.*
アメリカ合衆国のインターンシップ面接（ワシントン D.C.）　76

**Chapter 13**　*University and Dormitory Life in Sweden*
スウェーデンの科目留学と学生寮生活（ストックホルム）　82

**Chapter 14**　*Volunteer Work in the Philippines*
フィリピンのボランティア活動（フィリピン）　88

**Chapter 15**　*Around the World on a Volunteer Ship*
世界をめぐるボランティア活動（ボランティア船）　94

**Review Test Ⅲ**　　Chapter 12 － Chapter 15
コロケーション　100

**Phrase List** ─────────────── 102

# Chapter 1　*Home Stay in Canada (Yumi)*
### カナダの語学留学（バンクーバー）

ユミは初めて海外留学に出かけます。行先はカナダのバンクーバーです。どんなことが待ち受けているのでしょうか。

## I. Vocabulary Preview

本章で扱う語(句)です。それぞれの意味を表す日本語を選びなさい。

1. including     (　)  2. address    (　)  3. enroll     (　)
4. appropriate   (　)  5. online     (　)  6. obvious    (　)

> a. インターネットを通じて　　b. 手紙などを〜にあてて送る　　c. 適切な
> d. （講座など）に登録する　　e. 〜を含めて　　　　　　　　f. 出席する
> g. 明らかな

## II. Introduction

本章で扱う内容の紹介です。英文にさっと目を通して、次の問いに英語で答えなさい。　Track 2

> 　　Five students including Yumi Yamamoto joined their university's English study program in Canada. They left Japan on the evening of July 31st and arrived in Vancouver on the morning of the same day.
> 　　You will learn about a typical first day at a language school, gain knowledge about Canada, and understand what it can feel like to study abroad for the first time. Let's read her email report addressed to the International Center of their university.

(1) The students are going to Canada. What is the purpose of their trip?

(2) They left Japan on the evening of July 31st and arrived in Canada on the morning of the same day. How can such a thing happen?

## III. Reading

ユミのメールを読んで問いに答えなさい。

Track 3

 After about a nine-hour flight, we arrived in Canada yesterday morning! We took taxies from the airport to the English Language Institute of the University of British Columbia. They gave us a placement test as soon as we **enrolled in** the summer English program. They will put us into classes appropriate for us, based on our test scores. The first class starts on Monday, and we must arrive by 8:40 a.m.

 Our host families arrived to **pick us up** in the late afternoon. I recognized Mr. Brown, my host father, at once. We had already exchanged emails and photographs online. He was so kind and cheerful. He quickly put my baggage into the trunk of his car and we started off. It was a **twenty-minute drive** to their house. I was introduced to each family member and led to my room upstairs. That night, the family asked me a lot of questions about my life in Japan and about Japan in general. I realized that my life had **changed so much** in less than twenty-four hours. I am now living with a family that only speaks to me in English! I cannot experience this at home.

 Today, they took me on a tour of the city and told me about each place we visited. **It's obvious that** Vancouver is a very beautiful city and that my host family is friendly. During my stay in Canada, I'd like to not only improve my English but also make a lot of friends.

## 1. *Words & Phrases*

本文の太字の語句の中から適切なものを選んで空所に記入しなさい。

(1) "How far is it from here to the university?" "Well, it is about a (　　　　　　)."

(2) Yumi handed in her homework on time but she looks so tired. (　　　　　　) she had been writing it all night.

(3) "We've missed the bus, Mary."
　　"Don't worry, Yumi. My father will (　　　　　　) if we call."

(4) In addition to the summer program, I (　　　　　　) the Canadian lifestyle course.

(5) I met an old school friend after many years. However, I didn't recognise her at first because she had (　　　　　　).

## 2. *Grammar*

空所に適語を入れてそれぞれ 2 つの表現が同じような意味になるようにしなさい。

(1) A. After about a nine-hour flight, we arrived in Canada!
B. After we (　　) for about nine hours, we landed in Canada!

① flowed　　② flight　　③ flew　　④ fly

(2) A. I will study hard during my stay in Canada.
B. I am going to learn a lot (　　) I am in Canada.

① after　　② while　　③ time　　④ before

## 3. *Understanding the Text*

次の質問に英語で答えなさい。

(1) How long does it take to fly from Japan to Vancouver?
It takes _____.

(2) How does the English Language Institute put the students into appropriate classes?
It puts them in the classes based _____.

(3) Why did Yumi easily find Mr. Brown when they met for the first time?
Because they had already _____.

(4) What does Yumi think of her life with a family that speaks to her only in English?
_____.

(5) What does Yumi hope to do during her stay in Vancouver?
_____.

# IV. Listening

## 1. *Filling in the Blanks*

ユミがブラウン家の長男であるマーティンと話しています。CDを聴いて各空所に1語を入れなさい。

Track 4
Track 5

### Yumi and Martin's Conversation

| Part 1 | 1. Yumi _____ friends with some classmates. |
|        | 2. There are _____ classes before noon each day. |
|        | 3. The students are taught about the Canadian _____ in the afternoon. |
| Part 2 | 1. Vancouver is _____ to live in. |
|        | 2. Yumi feels _____ to be in Vancouver. |
|        | 3. You should be _____ in some areas of Vancouver. |

## 2. *Understanding the Dialog*

次は先ほどの会話の一部です。読んで、質問に答えなさい。

****************************************************************************

**From PART 1:** After the First Day in School

**Martin:** *How was school today? Have you made friends with your classmates?*

**Yumi:** *Oh, yes. I got to know a Mexican student, and a student from Spain.*

(1) At least how many nationalities are there in Yumi's class?

_____.

****************************************************************************

**From PART 2:** Talking about Vancouver

**Yumi:** *It sounds great. I'm very excited to be here.*

**Martin:** *I'm glad to hear that. However, please keep in mind that, like many other cities in the world, it has some areas where you should be careful.*

(2) What does Martin think about many cities in the world?

_____.

### Information Column: Donut Shops

カナダには Tim Hortons（ティム・ホートンズ）という人気のドーナッツ・チェーンがあります。カナダ発祥のお店で、多くのカナダ人が毎日利用するカナダの生活文化の定番です。甘いドーナッツとともに香り高いコーヒーが評判になっています。注文は "A medium coffee with milk and sugar, please." のように言います。このチェーン店で有名なのが "Double-Double" というフレーズ。ミルクと砂糖をそれぞれ 2 倍入れるという意味です。カナダに留学したら、ぜひ 1 度使ってみてください。

## V. Collocations

1. 語と語のつながりに注目して空所に最も適切な語を入れなさい。

(1) It cost Yumi a lot of money to go abroad. Before going to Canada, she worked part time and (　　　) some **money**.

① saved　　　② spent　　　③ brought　　　④ wasted
　A　　　　　　U　　　　　　E　　　　　　　I

(2) Yumi wants to improve her English. In other words, she wants to (　　　) **progress** with her English.

① do　　　② make　　　③ increase　　　④ fall
　Y　　　　　P　　　　　　G　　　　　　　W

(3) People who are good at communication can clearly express their opinions and also (　　　) **attention** to what others say.

① stand to　　② get　　　③ hear　　　④ pay
　N　　　　　　L　　　　　M　　　　　　K

(4) When Yumi doesn't understand some phrases in the newspaper, she sometimes (　　　) them **up** in her dictionary.

① sees　　　② finds　　　③ looks　　　④ checks
　I　　　　　A　　　　　　C　　　　　　E

2. 各正解選択肢の下にある赤色ローマ字を組み合わせて空所に入る単語を作りなさい。

"(　　　　　) your suitcase."

## 🌐 VI. Writing

下記はユミのブログの一部です。日本語に合うように下記の英文の続きを、与えられた語句を組み合せて完成しなさい。ただし、それぞれ1語を補い、文頭は大文字に直しなさい。

> カナダに初めて着いたときは少し不安でした。でも今は、以前より英語に自信があります。⑴学校で世界中からやって来ている学生と話すのはとても楽しいです。⑵ここにいる間にできるだけ多くのことを経験したい！

*I was a little nervous when I first arrived in Canada. Now, however, I have more confidence in my English than before.*

(1)　① the world at school　② with students　③ I greatly enjoy　④ from all over

_____.

(2)　① to experience as　② I want　③ many things as　④ while I am here

_____.

## 🌐 VII. What Can You Do Now?

最後に下記の3つの到達目標を読んで、できるものにチェックを入れなさい。

*I can*

☐ *understand the feelings I may have on my first study abroad trip.*

☐ *explain what I will be given on my first day at a language school.*

☐ *say something about Vancouver—a popular study abroad destination.*

# Chapter 2　*Home Stay in Australia (Masaru)*
## オーストラリアの語学留学（パース）

本章ではマサルが海外留学に出かけます。行先はオーストラリアのパースです。留学前の準備や留学後の生活に関しても語ります。

## I. Vocabulary Preview

本章で扱う語(句)です。それぞれの意味を表す日本語を選びなさい。

1. diligently　　　(　)　2. go downtown　(　)　3. get by　　　(　)
4. neighbourhood　(　)　5. chore　　　　(　)　6. conservation　(　)

| | | |
|---|---|---|
| a. なんとかやっていく | b. 雑用 | c. コツコツと |
| d. 繁華街に行く | e. 保護・保全 | f. 会話 |
| g. 近所 | | |

## II. Introduction

本章で扱う内容の紹介です。英文にさっと目を通して、次の問いに英語で答えなさい。　　Track 6

> Masaru has chosen to travel to Australia to learn English. He decided to stay in the city of Perth, in Western Australia. He flew from Japan to Hong Kong, and then from there to Perth. It was his first time on a plane, so it was very exciting.
>
> You will learn about life in Australia through his email report addressed to the International Centre of his university.

(1) Masaru flew from Japan to Hong Kong, and then to Perth. Why was it exciting for him?

(2) Why do you think Masaru chose to go to Australia to learn English?

# III. Reading

マサルのメールを読んで問いに答えなさい。  Track 7

About three weeks have passed since I came to Perth. I am **enjoying every moment** of my new life. After attending school, I often take pleasure in swimming or going downtown with my friends from Thailand and Vietnam. At night I **concentrate on** preparing for the next day's lessons. The people in my home stay family all live busy lives but, on the weekends, we **manage to** spend time together having a barbecue in the garden. This is my Australian life.

Before going abroad, I was given three tasks by the study abroad staff. One was to read and speak aloud when I **come across** common English expressions. Another was to learn about my home stay city. The final task was to practice introducing Japanese culture in English. Those tasks have really helped me to get by in my life here.

My Australian teacher also set me three goals to achieve during my stay. The first is to make friends with 30 people in three months. I'm almost halfway there! The second is to be **involved in** the community. The other day, I visited a school in my neighbourhood and introduced my hometown. The last goal is to keep a record of my trip in English. In fact, this is part of it.

My three aims after I return to Japan are to give a presentation of my experiences in Australia, to write a report about them, and finally to continue studying English diligently. I heard that many students stop learning after they finish studying abroad.

## 1. *Words & Phrases*

本文の太字の語句の中から適切なものを選んで空所に記入しなさい。

(1) When I read the magazine, I was surprised to (　　　　　) a picture of my teacher.

(2) When I was in Japan, I was (　　　　　) the volleyball club. Now, I often play it on the beach here in Australia.

(3) I went to see the latest 3D film in the cinema with my little brother. I was pleased to see him (　　　　　) of it.

(4) If we go by taxi, we can (　　　　　) get there on time.

(5) My neighbour likes loud music and, because of this, I find it difficult to (　　　　　) reading my book.

## 2. *Grammar*
空所に適語を入れてそれぞれ 2 つの表現が同じような意味になるようにしなさい。

(1) A. We moved to this town five years ago.
   B. Five years (　　) since my family moved to this town.
   ① have passed　　② had past　　③ pass　　④ are passing

(2) A. How long have you known Mr Johnson?
   B. When did you (　　) to know Mr Johnson?
   ① become　　② get　　③ have　　④ lead

## 3. *Understanding the Text*
次の質問に英語で答えなさい。

(1) How long has Masaru been in Perth?
   He has been there for _____.

(2) Who does Masaru often spend time with after school?
   He spends time with his _____.

(3) What has helped Masaru to get by in his life in Australia?
   The three tasks given _____.

(4) How many friends has Masaru made so far?
   _____.

(5) Masaru is going to give a presentation and write a report when he returns to Japan. What else does he aim to do?
   _____.

## IV. Listening

### 1. Filling in the Blanks

マサルがホストマザーのウィリアム夫人と話しています。CD を聴いて各空所に 1 語を入れなさい。

Track 8
Track 9

#### Masaru and Mrs Williams' Conversation

| Part 1 | 1. Masaru asks if there are any _____ he needs to know about. |
| --- | --- |
|  | 2. Water _____ is very important in Australia. |
|  | 3. Masaru says he'd like to take a bath and _____. |
| Part 2 | 1. Masaru will be careful not to _____ water. |
|  | 2. Masaru would be happy to be _____. |
|  | 3. The chores include helping to _____ the barbecue. |

### 2. Understanding the Dialog

次は先ほどの会話の一部です。読んで、質問に答えなさい。

*******************************************************************************

**From PART 1:** Homestay Rules

**Masaru:** I'd love to take a bath and relax as I did in Japan, but here that sounds difficult.

**Mrs Williams:** I'm sorry, Masaru, but we don't have a bath. Baths use over twice as much water as showers.

(1) Why isn't there a bath in Mrs Williams house?

_____.

*******************************************************************************

**From PART 2:** Household Chores

**Masaru:** Is there anything else I need to know?

**Mrs Williams:** All family members help with the housework. I would like to treat you like the rest of the family.

(2) What does Mrs Williams expect Masaru to do?

_____.

*Chapter 2 Home Stay in Australia (Masaru)*

### Information Column: Household Chores in Australia

　毎日の家事は、世界中どこでもめんどうな仕事です。オーストラリアの家庭では、親は子供たちに自分たちができる範囲で分担する 'pull their weight' ように言います。そのため、子供たちは積極的に料理、掃除、ベットメーキング、庭の手入れなどを手伝います。ホームステイをする学生も家事の分担を頼まれることがあります。

　これまで家事の内容は男女で分けられていました。男の子は家の外でフェンスのペンキ塗りや植木の剪定、女の子は料理や洗濯を任されました。しかし、最近では性別による分業はふさわしくないとの判断から家事を平等に振り分けようとしている家庭もあります。もし、ホームステイ先の家族から家事を頼まれたら、家族の一員として認められていると考えて、気軽に引き受けましょう。

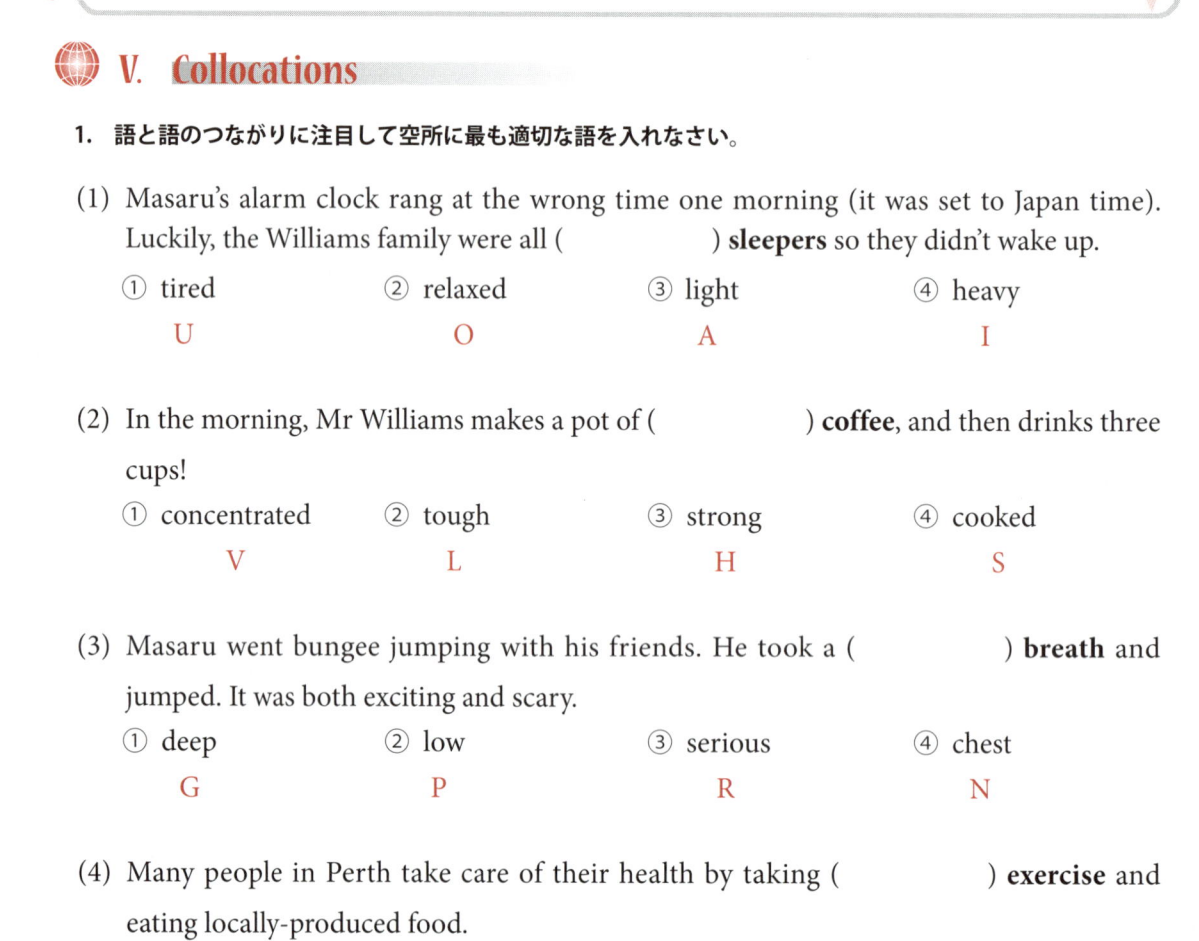

## V. Collocations

1. 語と語のつながりに注目して空所に最も適切な語を入れなさい。

(1) Masaru's alarm clock rang at the wrong time one morning (it was set to Japan time). Luckily, the Williams family were all (　　　　) **sleepers** so they didn't wake up.

① tired　　　② relaxed　　　③ light　　　④ heavy
　U　　　　　　　O　　　　　　　A　　　　　　I

(2) In the morning, Mr Williams makes a pot of (　　　　) **coffee**, and then drinks three cups!

① concentrated　　② tough　　③ strong　　④ cooked
　V　　　　　　　　　L　　　　　　H　　　　　　S

(3) Masaru went bungee jumping with his friends. He took a (　　　　) **breath** and jumped. It was both exciting and scary.

① deep　　　② low　　　③ serious　　　④ chest
　G　　　　　　P　　　　　　R　　　　　　　N

(4) Many people in Perth take care of their health by taking (　　　　) **exercise** and eating locally-produced food.

① always　　　② usual　　　③ regular　　　④ often
　M　　　　　　　J　　　　　　　H　　　　　　　W

2. 各正解選択肢の下にある赤色ローマ字を組み合わせて空所に入る単語を作りなさい。

'Australian dairy products are known for their (　　　　) quality and delicious taste'.

16　Let's Get Out of Japan!

## VI. Writing

下記はマサルのブログの一部です。日本語に合うように下記の英文の続きを、与えられた語句を組み合せて完成しなさい。ただし、それぞれ1語を補い、文頭は大文字に直しなさい。

> パースはオーストラリアの西海岸にあって、インド洋に面しています。だから思う存分ビーチに出かけることができます。(1) クラスの仲間たちが今週末、ビーチでパーティを催す準備をしています。(2) 私に加わるようにと誘ってくれたときは本当にうれしかったです。

*Perth is located on the west coast of Australia, facing the Indian Ocean. Therefore, I can go to the beach as often/much as I like!*

(1)　① a group　② my classmates are　③ party this weekend　④ organising a beach

_____.

(2)　① I was　② join them　③ they invited me　④ so happy when

_____.

## VII. What Can You Do Now?

最後に下記の3つの到達目標を読んで、できるものにチェックを入れなさい。

*I can*

☐ *give examples of aims or goals that students who go abroad might have.*

☐ *explain and give examples of rules that Australian families can have.*

☐ *say something about Perth in Australia.*

*Chapter 2 Home Stay in Australia (Masaru)*

# Chapter 3  *Home Stay in Britain (Kenta)*
## イギリスの語学留学（エジンバラ）

この章ではイギリスの北部に位置するスコットランドで学ぶ男子学生が登場します。彼は毎日、英語を学びながら英国のみならず、ヨーロッパ各地の文化や社会事情に関する知識も深めています。

## I. Vocabulary Preview

本章で扱う語（句）です。それぞれの意味を表す日本語を選びなさい。

1. economy (　　)  2. independent (　　)  3. local area (　　)
4. trend (　　)  5. make a difference (　　)  6. increase (　　)

| | | |
|---|---|---|
| a. 頻度 | b. 変化をもたらす | c. 地元 |
| d. 増加する | e. 経済 | f. 独立した |
| g. 傾向 | | |

## II. Introduction

本章で扱う内容の紹介です。英文にさっと目を通して、次の問いに英語で答えなさい。

Track 10

　　Kenta goes to an English language centre in the city of Edinburgh in Scotland, in the north of Britain. He will stay for four months. As he is majoring in economics, he hopes to visit some Japanese companies doing business there during his stay. His classmates are of many nationalities from around the world. Kenta tells us about an interesting conversation he had with European students. They talked about young people continuing to live with their parents.

(1) Kenta studies economics. What is he hoping to do during his stay in Britain?

(2) There are many European students in Kenta's class. Why do you think Britain is a popular study abroad destination for European students?

# III. Reading

ケンタの報告を読んで問いに答えなさい。   Track 11

> I've been here for one month now and I'm enjoying my life very much. Scottish people have **a good sense of humour** and speak with a lively accent. There are many different nationalities in my language school, including people from Denmark, Slovakia (in Central Europe), and Finland. I'm happy to be able to learn not only about Britain and British people, but also about the lives of people in other European countries.
>
> We had an interesting conversation **the other day** during **lunch break**. I said that, in Japan, I live alone in a rented apartment near my university and, if I find a job in my hometown after graduation, I plan to move back to my parents' home. A Danish woman was surprised that I would consider living with my parents again. She said that, in Denmark, young people are expected to move out of home and become independent as soon as they can. A Slovakian man, however, said **that is not the case** in his country. He told us that many young people these days continue to live at home with their parents. Anyway, we all agreed that, **due to** bad economic conditions, the number of young people living with parents has been increasing in recent years in many countries.
>
> I have learned that young people are encouraged to move out of home and become independent in some countries, while they are expected to stay with their parents in others. In any case, however, their lifestyles are greatly influenced by economic and social situations.

## 1. *Words & Phrases*

本文の太字の語句の中から適切なものを選んで空所に記入しなさい。

(1) My French friend makes me laugh and smile every time we meet. She is really a nice person with (　　　　　　　).

(2) I thought that all English people prefer tea to coffee, but I realised (　　　　　　　) when my English friend told me that he drinks coffee more often.

(3) 'Have you seen John recently? He hasn't come to class for weeks'!
'Yes, I saw him (　　　　　　　) at the train station. He had a nice suntan. Do you think he had been on holiday'?

(4) All trains were cancelled yesterday (　　　　　　　) the heavy snow.

(5) I promised to meet Maria at (　　　　　　　), but I forgot. I wonder if she is angry at me now.

## 2. *Grammar*

**空所に適語を入れてそれぞれ 2 つの表現が同じような意味になるようにしなさい。**

(1) A. More and more young people have begun to live with their parents in Japan.
   B. In Japan, the number of young people (　　) with their parents has been increasing year by year.
   ① live　　　② living　　　③ lived　　　④ to live

(2) A. I'm sorry I can't lend you this because it is a library book.
   B. This is a book (　　) from the library, so I can't lend it to you.
   ① borrowed　　　② to borrow　　　③ borrow　　　④ borrowing

## 3. *Understanding the Text*

**次の質問に英語で答えなさい。**

(1) According to Kenta, how do Scottish people speak?
   They speak with _____.

(2) What was Kenta happy to learn about?
   He was happy to learn about Britain and British people, and _____.

(3) Why was the Danish woman surprised when she heard Kenta might live with his parents again?
   In her country, young people are _____.

(4) In what way is Slovakia different from Denmark these days?
   _____.

(5) What did everyone agree?
   _____.

# IV. Listening

## 1. *Filling in the Blanks*

ケンタがホームステイ先のブレイクさんと話しています。CD を聴いて各空所に 1 語を入れなさい。

Track 12
Track 13

### Kenta and Mr Blake's Conversation

| Part 1 | 1. Young people in Denmark _____ to move out early. |
|        | 2. Countries in northern Europe show a similar _____. |
|        | 3. Young people in the other parts of Europe _____ to stay at home longer. |
| Part 2 | 1. The economy in the _____ countries has been stronger in recent years. |
|        | 2. Young people find it easier to get a _____ when the economy is strong. |
|        | 3. Kenta feels that there is _____ reason. |

## 2. *Understanding the Dialog*

次は先ほどの会話の一部です。読んで、質問に答えなさい。

**From PART 1:** Different Cultures

**Kenta:** *I found out that young people in Denmark tend to move out of the family home early.*

**Mr Blake:** *Yes, there is such a trend in northern Europe.*

(1) What trend exists in northern Europe?

_____.

**From PART 2:** Mr Blake's Opinion

**Kenta:** *Why would the economy make a difference, Mr Blake?*

**Mr Blake:** *A strong economy makes it easier for young people to get a job. Then, they can become independent.*

(2) What can happen to young people when they get a job?

_____.

### Information Column: Afternoon Tea

英国には 'Afternoon Tea' という習慣があります。午後3時ごろから紅茶とともにサンドイッチやデザート類をいただきます。スコットランドでは 'High Tea' という呼び方のほうが有名で、夕方にサンドイッチやスコーンのほか、パイ等も食べることがあります。街のレストランでは、様々な種類の紅茶やケーキ類を堪能できます。個人の家庭に招待されたときは、積極的に会話に参加して、楽しいティー・タイムを過ごしましょう。'Homemade cake' を提供してくれるかもしれません。

## V. Collocations

1. 語と語のつながりに注目して空所に最も適切な語を入れなさい。

   (1) Kenta may (　　　　) **a job** in the local area after graduating from university.
   
   　① select　　　　② get　　　　③ receive　　　　④ pick
   　　A　　　　　　　O　　　　　　I　　　　　　　U

   (2) Some young people stay at home to (　　　　) **care** of their parents.
   
   　① get　　　　② do　　　　③ take　　　　④ grab
   　　R　　　　　　N　　　　　　L　　　　　　W

   (3) After graduating, some young people (　　　　) stay**ing** in the family home to save money.
   
   　① plan　　　　② expect　　　　③ think　　　　④ consider
   　　P　　　　　　W　　　　　　　V　　　　　　　T

   (4) Kenta (　　　　) **to the conclusion** that there are many reasons for young people choosing to live at home with their parents.
   
   　① came　　　　② saw　　　　③ ran　　　　④ went
   　　S　　　　　　T　　　　　　C　　　　　　H

2. 各正解選択肢の下にある赤色ローマ字を組み合わせて空所に入る単語を作りなさい。

   '(　　　　　) and Found'

## VI. Writing

下記はケンタのブログの一部です。日本語に合うように下記の英文の続きを、与えられた語句を組み合せて完成しなさい。。ただし、それぞれ1語を補い、文頭は大文字に直しなさい。

> 私たちはエディンバラの西にあるグラスゴーに行く予定です。私は音楽祭に出かけるのを心待ちにしています。(1) 夜は若者の間で人気のあるクラブに出かけて、みんなで楽しく過ごしたいです。(2) バスで行くか、電車で行くか、みんなで思案中です。

*A group of us is going to travel to Glasgow, a city to the west of Edinburgh. I am looking forward to going to a music festival.*

(1)　① nightclub popular　② enjoy ourselves at a　③ young people　④ at night, we want to

_____.

(2)　① we will travel there　② or train　③ we are wondering　④ by bus

_____.

## VII. What Can You Do Now?

最後に下記の3つの到達目標を読んで、できるものにチェックを入れなさい。

*I can*

☐ *give an example of a difference that European countries have.*

☐ *say something about a custom that British people have.*

☐ *feel more confident with commonly used words, phrases and collocations.*

# Chapter 4    *Internship in Singapore (Miki)*
シンガポールのインターンシップ体験（シンガポール）

以前の海外語学研修で英語に磨きをかけたミキが、今回ワーキングホリデイの制度を使い、シンガポールでインターシップを体験します。派遣先は日本の大手銀行のシンガポール支店です。

## I. Vocabulary Preview

本章で扱う語（句）です。それぞれの意味を表す日本語を選びなさい。

1. innovative (　　) 　2. immigrate (　　) 　3. approach (　　)
4. especially (　　) 　5. destination (　　) 　6. take advantage of (　　)

- a. 祖先
- b. 刷新的な
- c. 移民する
- d. 取り組み
- e. 特に
- f. 目的地
- g. 利用する

## II. Introduction

本章で扱う内容の紹介です。英文にさっと目を通して、次の問いに英語で答えなさい。　Track 14

> Miki is a university student majoring in finance. She has studied English abroad before so, this time, she is going on a working holiday. She will work at the Singapore branch of a large Japanese bank for six months. Miki takes advantage of the opportunity of working in Singapore to learn about life outside Japan, especially in other Asian countries.

(1) At least how long will Miki stay in Singapore?

(2) What do you think Miki will experience in Singapore?

## III. Reading

ミキの報告を読んで問いに答えなさい。　　　　　　　　　Track 15

　　I arrived in Singapore two weeks ago. I work in the public relations section of a bank where I put information for Japanese-speaking clients on its website. I work with five people of different ethnic backgrounds, and I've already made friends with all of them. In particular, I enjoy **spending time** with Peter, a twenty-five-year-old man from Sweden, and Lina, a twenty-two-year-old Chinese woman.

　　Lina's family immigrated to Singapore when she was three years old. She told me that she speaks Chinese at home and uses English at work. According to her, over 70% of Singapore's residents are ethnic Chinese, followed by Malays and Indians. Children here start learning English from when they enter elementary school. You can make yourself understood in English anywhere. This surely helps make it easy for foreign people to live here. About **one in three** people living in Singapore are foreigners. They come from all over the world including, of course, Japan. It is really **a multi-ethnic society.**

　　**As you know**, my university major is finance. This working holiday is giving me a lot of valuable experience. It is also an **ideal way** for me to learn about issues companies have when staff members are from many different countries. One advantage of having a multicultural workforce is that they have many interesting ideas. However, on the other hand, many people tend to leave their jobs after only a couple of years. They often return to their own countries, or move to another company in Singapore for better working conditions.

## 1. Words & Phrases

本文の太字の語句の中から適切なものを選んで空所に記入しなさい。

(1) I wonder how schools provide equal and fair education for students in (　　　　　　　　　).

(2) Food culture has been changing in recent years. It is said that (　　　　　　　　　) people in Japan don't eat breakfast regularly these days.

(3) 'I heard all about your illness from your brother! Are you OK now'?
　　'I'm fine now, thanks. (　　　　　　　　　), I had a high fever for three days'!

(4) Some teachers say that the (　　　　　　　　　) to learn a language is to use it in everyday life.

(5) Since my father and mother retired, they have been (　　　　　　　　　) with each other more than ever before.

## 2. *Grammar*
空所に適語を入れてそれぞれ 2 つの表現が同じような意味になるようにしなさい。

(1) A. Until recently, most people completely trusted what doctors said.
　　B. In the past, it was unusual (　　　　) ordinary people to see another doctor to get a second opinion.

　　① of　　　　② that　　　　③ to　　　　④ for

(2) A. I appreciate it that you answered my e-mail and advised me.
　　B. It was kind (　　　　) you to respond to my e-mail and give me your opinion.

　　① of　　　　② that　　　　③ to　　　　④ for

## 3. *Understanding the Text*
次の質問に英語で答えなさい。

(1) According to Miki, when did she arrive in Singapore?
　　She arrived _____.

(2) Is there any evidence that Singapore is a multi-ethnic society?
　　Yes, there is. Over 70% of people are ethnic Chinese, _____.

(3) What makes it easy for foreign people to go to Singapore, according to Lina?
　　You can make yourself understood _____.

(4) Why do you think Miki was interested in a working holiday at a bank in Singapore?
　　_____.

(5) What can be a disadvantage of having a multinational workforce, according to Miki?
　　_____.

# IV. Listening

## 1. Filling in the Blanks

ミキが同じ職場にいるピーターさんと話しています。CD を聴いて各空所に 1 語を入れなさい。

Track 16
Track 17

### Miki and Peter's Conversation

| Part 1 | 1. Miki went to the _____ store to buy some chewing gum. |
| --- | --- |
| | 2. The Singapore government does not allow chewing gum to be _____. |
| | 3. In the past, chewing gum made the _____ dirty. |
| Part 2 | 1. _____ on the street is also against the law. |
| | 2. Peter says you could be _____ 1,000 Singapore dollars. |
| | 3. Miki feels that the rules in Singapore are _____. |

## 2. Understanding the Dialog

次は先ほどの会話の一部です。読んで、質問に答えなさい。

*********************************************************************************

**From PART 1:** Law and Order

**Peter:** *It is very difficult to buy chewing gum in Singapore. The government does not allow it to be imported into the country.*

**Miki:** *Why? Chewing gum keeps my teeth clean and my breath fresh.*

(1) Why does Miki think chewing gum is beneficial?

_____.

*********************************************************************************

**From PART 2:** Strict Rules

**Miki:** *In Japan, people sometimes cross the road at the wrong place. The rules in Singapore sound very strict.*

**Peter:** *They might be. However, such strict rules are good for the safety and comfort of society, I believe.*

(2) Why does Peter agree with Singapore's strict rules?

_____.

*Chapter 4 Internship in Singapore (Miki)* **27**

## ✈ Information Column: Amazing Singapore

シンガポールはおよそ淡路島ほどの大きさです。そこに国民の７割以上を占める中国系のほか、マライ系、インド系など人々が暮らし、さらに労働人口の３割を超える数の外国人労働者が同居する多民族・多国籍社会です。街のあちこちに各民族が集まる地区があり、食事や買い物をする憩いの場所も存在しています。チャイナ・タウンはもちろん、インドやバングラディシュ出身者で賑わうリトル・インディア、マレーシアやインドネシア出身者が通うアラブ・ストリートなどはよく知られています。近代的なビル群とエスニックな雰囲気を漂わせている街並みとの対比がとても興味深いです。日系のレストランやデパートも多数進出していますが、使用言語は英語が基本です。

## 🌐 V. Collocations

**1.** 語と語のつながりに注目して空所に最も適切な語を入れなさい。

(1) It is said that Singapore has (　　　　) **economy**.
　① a building　　② an increasing　　③ a thriving　　④ a creating
　　　I　　　　　　　　E　　　　　　　　A　　　　　　　O

(2) Singapore often (　　　　) **events** for locals and tourists to enjoy.
　① holds　　② grasps　　③ carries　　④ keeps
　　　A　　　　　E　　　　　U　　　　　I

(3) Companies that take an **innovative** (　　　　) problems are often successful.
　① method with　　② tactic for　　③ methodology　　④ approach to
　　　R　　　　　　　B　　　　　　　T　　　　　　　S

(4) There are so many people with different backgrounds living together in Singapore. In other words, it is a (　　　　) **bowl** of various cultures.
　① tea　　② dessert　　③ coffee　　④ salad
　　U　　　　O　　　　　E　　　　　I

**2.** 各正解選択肢の下にある赤色ローマ字を組み合わせて空所に入る単語を作りなさい。

　Singapore is one of the most successful countries in Southeast (　　　　　　).

*Let's Get Out of Japan!*

## VI. Writing

下記はミキのブログの一部です。日本語に合うように下記の英文の続きを、与えられた語句を組み合せて完成しなさい。ただし、それぞれ1語を補い、文頭は大文字に直しなさい。

> 昨日、友人のリナの家に招待されました。彼女の両親は中国系ですが、英語を上手に話します。(1) 出された食事は、中国料理、インド料理、西洋料理が混ざり合ったものでした。(2) シンガポールの多文化社会が、人々の日々のくらしに影響を与えています。

*I was invited to my friend Lina's house for dinner yesterday. Lina's parents are ethnic Chinese, but they speak English very well.*

(1)　① the meal served　② was a　③ and Western food　④ of Chinese, Indian

_____ .

(2)　① Singapore's　② society　③ daily lives　④ affects people's

_____ .

## VII. What Can You Do Now?

最後に下記の3つの到達目標を読んで、できるものにチェックを入れなさい。

<u>*I can*</u>

☐ *say an advantage and a disadvantage of having a multicultural workforce.*

☐ *give some examples of laws in Singapore.*

☐ *talk about Singaporean society.*

# Chapter 5　*Home Stay in Ireland (Maria)*
## アイルランドの語学留学（ダブリン）

この章は女子学生のマリアが、アイルランド（共和国）に出かけます。アイルランドはイギリスの西に位置する島国で、長い歴史を持つ国です。

## I. Vocabulary Preview

本章で扱う語（句）です。それぞれの意味を表す日本語を選びなさい。

1. via          (　　)　2. delighted     (　　)　3. immigration   (　　)
4. trolley      (　　)　5. arrivals gate (　　)　6. loft          (　　)

> a. 屋根裏部屋　　b. 到着ゲート　　c. 一時停止
> d. 押し車　　　　e. 〜経由で　　　f. 入国審査
> g. うれしい

## II. Introduction

本章で扱う内容の紹介です。英文にさっと目を通して、次の問いに英語で答えなさい。

Track 18

> Maria is a university student majoring in history. She is especially interested in European history. However, she is also interested in learning English. She has been interested in English since she first started learning the language. She is very happy to travel to Ireland because she knows that Ireland has a long and varied history. She will stay with a host family in the capital city, Dublin. Let's find out what she learns in Ireland!

(1) What two things is Maria interested in?

(2) Why do you think Maria would like to stay with a local family?

## III. Reading

マリアのメール報告を読んで問いに答えなさい。　　　　　　　　　　　Track 19

> There is no **direct flight** from Japan to Ireland, so I flew via London. The colour of the plane to Ireland was green! I got my first taste of Ireland on the plane when we were served Irish brown bread, butter and cheese. Irish **dairy products** are delicious.
>
> On the plane, all announcements were made in two languages. I understood the English, but I wondered what the other language was. The lady sitting next to me kindly explained that, while Irish people speak English, they also have a different language called Irish. For example, 'How are you'? is 'Conas atá tú'? (注1) in Irish. I had already begun learning about Ireland, even though I hadn't arrived yet!
>
> After arriving at Dublin airport, I showed my passport at immigration and answered the questions I was asked. Then, I collected my **check-in luggage** from the conveyor belt. I also had one piece of **carry-on luggage**, so I used a trolley, or cart, to make it easier to carry them. My host family met me at the arrivals gate. I had been worried, so I was delighted and relieved when they **welcomed me with** a hug. I told them that I was very happy to stay with them.
>
> I am writing this in my room. It is a pretty room in the loft with a bathroom. I have just woken up after a 12-hour sleep (I was very tired, and the bed was so comfortable), and I am looking forward to eating my first Irish breakfast.

(注1) 発音は：(kənəs ataː tuː)

## 1. *Words & Phrases*

本文の太字の語句の中から適切なものを選んで空所に記入しなさい。

(1) I was surprised to hear that my friend is allergic to (　　　　　　　) such as milk, butter and cheese.

(2) Many people like to go by (　　　　　　　) as they don't have to change planes. However, a connecting flight can often be cheaper.

(3) I remember visiting my grandmother's house when I was a child. In summer, she (　　　　　　　) a slice of watermelon.

(4) Many airlines have strict rules about the size and weight of (　　　　　　　). If it is too big, you have to check it in.

(5) It is not recommended to put cash or other valuables in your (                              ) in case it gets lost.

## 2. *Grammar*
空所に適語を入れてそれぞれ 2 つの表現が同じような意味になるようにしなさい。

(1) A. Maria wrote an email and her host mother made breakfast at the same time.
   B. (       ) Maria was writing her email, her host mother prepared breakfast.
   ① After　　　　② As soon as　　　　③ Although　　　　④ While

(2) A. Maria saw her host mother putting plates on the table when she went downstairs.
   B. (       ) Maria went downstairs to have breakfast, she noticed her host mother setting the table.
   ① Although　　　② As soon as　　　　③ As　　　　　　　④ Before

## 3. *Understanding the Text*
次の質問に英語で答えなさい。

(1) Why did Maria fly to Ireland via London?
   There is no _____.

(2) What food was served on the plane from London to Ireland?
   The passengers were served _____.

(3) In what languages were the announcements on the plane made?
   They were made in _____.

(4) Why did Maria use a trolley at Dublin Airport?
   _____.

(5) Why is Maria interested in studying in Ireland? (See the Introduction)
   _____.

## IV. Listening

### 1. *Filling in the Blanks*

マリアが大学生のパトリックと話しています。CD を聴いて各空所に 1 語を入れなさい。

Track 20
Track 21

#### Maria and Patrick's Conversation

| Part 1 | 1. The people Maria heard on the _____ weren't speaking in English. |
|---|---|
| | 2. Poland is a country in _____ Europe. |
| | 3. Polish is the second most _____ language in Ireland. |
| Part 2 | 1. Ireland's economy was _____ at the beginning of the 21st century. |
| | 2. Ireland needed more _____. |
| | 3. Irish people now have a more _____ point of view. |

### 2. *Understanding the Dialog*

次は先ほどの会話の一部です。読んで、質問に答えなさい。

\*\*\*\*\*\*\*\*\*\*\*\*\*\*\*\*\*\*\*\*\*\*\*\*\*\*\*\*\*\*\*\*\*\*\*\*\*\*\*\*\*\*\*\*\*\*\*\*\*\*\*\*\*\*\*\*\*\*\*\*\*\*\*\*\*\*\*\*\*\*\*\*\*\*\*

**From PART 1:** Multilingual

**Maria:** *Why is Polish spoken in Ireland? That country is so far from here!*

**Patrick:** *After Poland joined the European Union in 2004, many Polish people came to Ireland to find work.*

(1) What occurred before many Polish people went to Ireland to find work?

_____.

\*\*\*\*\*\*\*\*\*\*\*\*\*\*\*\*\*\*\*\*\*\*\*\*\*\*\*\*\*\*\*\*\*\*\*\*\*\*\*\*\*\*\*\*\*\*\*\*\*\*\*\*\*\*\*\*\*\*\*\*\*\*\*\*\*\*\*\*\*\*\*\*\*\*\*

**From PART 2:** Change in Society

**Maria:** *Did society change after so many foreign people arrived?*

**Patrick:** *Yes, of course! We have learned so many things from the new arrivals. Thanks to that, the way we look at the world has changed.*

(2) Why has the way Irish people look at the world changed?

_____.

*Chapter 5 Home Stay in Ireland (Maria)*

### Information Column: A Changing Ireland

　アイルランドはヨーロッパの西に位置する島国です。9000年前ごろに初めて人が住み始めたと言われています。紀元前3世紀ごろからケルト系の人々が大陸から渡り、アイルランドの豊かな文化と伝統を築いてきました。アイルランド人はアイルランド語を話しましたが、近世になって英国の支配を受けると英語が幅広く使用されるようになりました。

　近年、その言語環境に大きな変化が起こりつつあります。18世紀から20世紀半ばまで多くのアイルランド人が仕事を求めて英国、アメリカ、オーストラリアに移住したことは、歴史上よく知られています。1990年代から今日にかけて、アイルランドの経済状況が向上すると、ヨーロッパ各地、アフリカ、アジアからの移民者が急増しました。今やポーランド語が英語についで2番目に多く話されている言語になっています。

## V. Collocations

**1.** 語と語のつながりに注目して空所に最も適切な語を入れなさい。

(1) Many Irish people can (　　　　) more than one **language**.

　① talk　　　　② speak　　　　③ say　　　　④ discuss
　　P　　　　　　　T　　　　　　　N　　　　　　C

(2) Some people like to (　　　　) **the television** during dinner and chat with their family.

　① push off　　② turn off　　③ put off　　④ press off
　　R　　　　　　L　　　　　　Y　　　　　　S

(3) Irish people tend to (　　　　) **a shower** in the morning, instead of a bath at night.

　① bring　　② clean　　③ wash　　④ have
　　V　　　　　G　　　　　H　　　　　L

(4) In Ireland, Irish and Polish people work well together, showing that people of different cultures can (　　　　) **their trust in** each other.

　① make　　② get　　③ put　　④ pour
　　I　　　　　A　　　　E　　　　U

**2.** 各正解選択肢の下にある赤色ローマ字を組み合わせて空所に入る単語を作りなさい。

　People in Ireland like to (　　　　) traditional stories to one another.

Let's Get Out of Japan!

## VI. Writing

下記はマリアのブログの一部です。日本語に合うように下記の英文の続きを、与えられた語句を組み合せて完成しなさい。ただし、それぞれ1語を補い、文頭は大文字に直しなさい。

> 私はここで英語だけでなく歴史や文化も学んでいます。来週は伝統音楽祭に友人と出かけます。⑴ アイルランドの西方にあるいくつかの古城も訪れるつもりです。⑵ そこからは田園の景色が一望できます。

*I'm learning not only English but also history and culture here. Next week, I will go to a traditional music festival with my friends.*

(1)　① we will also　② some old castles　③ of Ireland　④ in the west

_____.

(2)　① of the　② panoramic views　③ from there, you　④ can enjoy

_____.

## VII. What Can You Do Now?

最後に下記の3つの到達目標を読んで、できるものにチェックを入れなさい。

*I can*

☐ *talk about the languages used in Ireland.*

☐ *give an example of how Ireland has changed recently.*

☐ *give some possible reasons why someone would be interested in studying in Ireland.*

# Chapter 6　*Internship Program in the USA (Kazu)*
## アメリカ合衆国のインターンシップ体験（ワシントンD.C.）

ワシントンD.C. には、国内外で活躍しているNGO（non-governmental organization）やNPO（non-profit organization）が多数存在します。今回、カズはあるNGOのワシントン支部で行っている奉仕活動について報告します。

## I. Vocabulary Preview

本章で扱う語（句）です。それぞれの意味を表す日本語を選びなさい。

1. organization (　　)　2. internship (　　)　3. transform (　　)
4. institution (　　)　5. dignity (　　)　6. initiative (　　)

> a. 一変させる　　　　b. 地域社会　　　　　　　　c. 体面
> d. 組織　　　　　　　e. （大学・銀行などの）機関　f. 自発性
> g. インターンシップ

## II. Introduction

本章で扱う内容の紹介です。英文にさっと目を通して、次の問いに英語で答えなさい。　　Track 22

> An internship program allows students to discover and develop their interests. Students can work in many types of businesses, including well-known companies and non-governmental organizations (NGOs). However, they are usually not paid for their work.
> 
> In this chapter, we will learn about an internship program which provides both study and work opportunities. Kazu, a junior majoring in social welfare, is now studying at a university in Washington D.C., taking a course called Transforming Communities.

(1) What does an internship program allow?

(2) Why do you think Kazu is taking a course called Transforming Communities?

## III. Reading

カズのメールを読んで問いに答えなさい。　　　　Track 23

As you know, I am now studying in Washington D.C. on a college internship program. The programs offered in Washington D.C. are well known and popular at **home and abroad**, because you have a chance to work for various international organizations or public institutions such as art galleries or museums. There are also a few hundred NGOs working for people **in need of** assistance. I **applied for** this internship program to join such an NGO. This is because I'd like to learn more about problems in society and understand how to solve them.

Let me tell you about my weekly schedule. On Mondays and Wednesdays we have lectures and debates at university about social issues. Then, on Fridays, we invite guest speakers and have a discussion. On Tuesdays and Thursdays, from noon to 6 p.m., I work for Bread and Blanket, an NGO. It provides the poor with clothes and freshly cooked food. We are taught to treat the poor as clients, i.e., to treat them with respect. We bag and distribute food to our clients twice a day, at noon and in the evening. At other times we sort donated clothes and **arrange them neatly** so our clients can select what they need with dignity.

Poverty in Washington D.C., the capital of the USA, is a very serious problem. I learned that well-paid jobs are occupied by **college graduates**, while people with low-level education and skills are forced to take the poorly paid ones. Through this internship, I can learn about the realities of the world.

## 1. Words & Phrases

本文の太字の語句の中から適切なものを選んで空所に記入しなさい。

(1) Although Japan is a rich country, some people are (　　　　　　　) food and shelter.

(2) I usually take my pencils out and (　　　　　　　) on the desk before a test.

(3) These days, it is difficult even for (　　　　　　　) to find secure jobs in Japan.

(4) Japanese inventions such as instant coffee are popular both at (　　　　　　　).

(5) I (　　　　　　　) a part-time job in a cafe, and I was asked to attend an interview the following day.

## 2. *Grammar*

空所に適語を入れてそれぞれ 2 つの表現が同じような意味になるようにしなさい。

(1) A. That company puts water into bottles.
B. That company (　　) water.
① ducks　　　② wraps　　　③ boxes　　　④ bottles

(2) A. Our group decided to stop thinking about that problem for a while.
B. We decided to let that problem (　　).
① skin　　　② screen　　　③ slide　　　④ snake

## 3. *Understanding the Text*

次の質問に英語で答えなさい。

(1) Why does Kazu want to work for an NGO?
He would like to learn about _____.

(2) How many hours per week does Kazu work for Bread and Blanket?
He works for _____.

(3) How does Bread and Blanket get the clothes that their clients are given?
The clothes are _____.

(4) What problem does Washington D.C. have?
_____.

(5) What can help Kazu learn about the realities of the world?
_____.

## IV. Listening

### 1. *Filling in the Blanks*

カズが **Bread and Blanket** のマネージャー、アンナさんと話しています。CD を聴いて各空所に 1 語を入れなさい。

Track 24
Track 25

#### Kazu and Anna's Conversation

| Part 1 | 1. Bread and Blanket helps _____ of clients every day. |
| --- | --- |
|  | 2. Anna doesn't want to use the term " _____ people." |
|  | 3. Bread and Blanket _____ services to clients. |
| Part 2 | 1. Kazu hasn't found any _____ to do. |
|  | 2. Anna wants Kazu to use his _____. |
|  | 3. Anna reminds Kazu to _____ the clients. |

### 2. *Understanding the Dialog*

次は先ほどの会話の一部です。読んで、質問に答えなさい。

*********************************************************************************

**From PART 1:** Treat with Respect

**Kazu:** *How many poor people do you help every day?*

**Anna:** *Oh, we serve hundreds of people, of all ages. By the way, we don't call them "poor people"; we call them "clients."*

(1) Does Bread and Blanket help only elderly people?

_____.

*********************************************************************************

**From PART 2:** Using Initiative

**Anna:** *Kazu, I want you to use your initiative. Look around and find work that needs to be done.*

**Kazu:** *There is a line of clients over there waiting to be served. I think I'll help at that counter.*

(2) What work does Anna tell Kazu to do?

_____.

*Chapter 6 Internship Program in the USA (Kazu)* **39**

### ✈ **Information Column: The Past and Present of Washington D.C.**

　アメリカ合衆国（the United States of America）は現在 50 州から成りますが、首都であるワシントン D.C. はその中に含まれていません。D.C. は District of Columbia（コロンビア特別区）の略で、1790 年に誕生しました。多数の政府機関や国際機関はもちろん、すばらしい博物館や記念館が市内各地に存在し、毎年多くの観光客が訪れます。

　信じがたいことですが、ワシントン D.C. は貧富の差が激しい都市でもあります。高給を得る人々がいる一方、日々の生活もままならない貧困層の人々が多数います。教育不足により就業する機会を得られないことが原因の 1 つです。一説によれば、2 割近い市民が英語で十分に読み書きができないと言われています。

## 🌐 V. Collocations

**1.** 語と語のつながりに注目して空所に最も適切な語を入れなさい。

(1) Kazu used to play computer games on weekends when he was younger. However, now he spends his (　　　　) **time** visiting museums and galleries.

　① bored　　　② free　　　③ used　　　④ open
　　　I　　　　　　E　　　　　　A　　　　　　U

(2) People who fall into poverty are sometimes helped by the (　　　　) **system**.

　① computer　② writing　③ welfare　④ automatic
　　　N　　　　　　W　　　　　T　　　　　　P

(3) If you do not understand the locals, it may be because of a (　　　　) **barrier**.

　① word　　② language　③ vocabulary　④ conversation
　　　O　　　　　A　　　　　　I　　　　　　　E

(4) Kazu would like to (　　　　) **the needs of** the clients of the NGO.

　① speak　　② read　　③ meet　　④ trace
　　　I　　　　　A　　　　　K　　　　　E

**2.** 各正解選択肢の下にある赤色ローマ字を組み合わせて空所に入る単語を作りなさい。

"(　　　　) up a job offer"

## VI. Writing

下記はカズのブログの一部です。日本語に合うように下記の英文の続きを、与えられた語句を組み合せて完成しなさい。ただし、それぞれ1語を補い、文頭は大文字に直しなさい。

> ワシントンD.C.は多くの相反する要素を持つ都市です。裕福な人々がいる一方で、貧しく暮らす人たちがいます。(1) しかし、博物館はたいていは無料なので、だれでも楽しむことができます。(2) 私は街を歩き回って歴史的な建物を見るのが好きです。

**Washington D.C. is a city of many contrasts. Some people here are rich, while others live in poverty.**

(1)　① however, in general,　② the museums are　③ can enjoy them　④ so anyone

_____.

(2)　① and looking at　② the historical　③ I enjoy walking　④ around the city

_____.

## VII. What Can You Do Now?

最後に下記の3つの到達目標を読んで、できるものにチェックを入れなさい。

_I can_

☐ *discuss some benefits of internship programs.*

☐ *understand reasons for the gap between rich and poor in a city in the USA.*

☐ *talk about Washington D.C.*

# Review Test I
## Chapters 1-6

*Choose the most suitable word or phrase for each blank space.*

1. Studying abroad can help you to …… knowledge about the world.
    A. change        B. gain        C. introduce        D. locate

2. I wasn't making …… by myself, so I decided to study together with my friends.
    A. progress        B. vocabulary        C. purpose        D. phrase

3. My mother …… my sister up from school because it was raining heavily.
    A. packed        B. took        C. stood        D. picked

4. I am very busy. I study hard at university and I also …… part time.
    A. employ        B. job        C. endure        D. work

5. The people who were …… the project are responsible for its failure.
    A. involved out        B. involved in        C. involved for        D. involved of

6. Buying …… food is good for the regional economy as it provides employment.
    A. locally-produced    B. globally-constructed    C. factory-made    D. nationally-sold

7. Taking …… exercise and eating healthily are ways to keep your body in shape.
    A. often        B. balanced        C. mental        D. regular

8. Even when I was a child, my father listened to my opinions and …… me as an equal.
    A. took        B. treated        C. made        D. conserved

9. I came to the …… that I wasn't destined to be a lawyer when I failed the examination for the third time.
    A. condition        B. conclusion        C. destination        D. result

10. Many students …… studying abroad when they realise how much it will teach them about the world.
    A. think        B. consider        C. decide        D. encourage

11. The book I borrowed from the library …… was very interesting. I recommend you read it.
    A. the other day        B. one more week        C. in a month        D. a long time

12. Not all people who …… medicine become doctors. There are many other jobs in which such knowledge can be useful.
    A. take on        B. study for        C. maximum at        D. major in

13. Participating in neighborhood events is an …… to make a connection with the local area.
    A. excellent road    B. ideal way    C. alternative path    D. ancient street

14. Any …… you take to learning a language will have its strengths and weaknesses.
    A. appreciate    B. achievement    C. approach    D. advance

15. There are many people in Brazil who have a Japanese ethnic …….
    A. background    B. minority    C. group    D. culture

16. A restaurant waiter is responsible for …… food and communicating with customers, among other tasks.
    A. serving    B. eating    C. waiting    D. giving

17. My ideal job is one where the salary is high and the …… are excellent.
    A. overtime situations    B. rival companies    C. working conditions    D. average colleagues

18. I got my first …… of success when I was able to speak to a foreigner in English.
    A. talk    B. touch    C. taste    D. tongue

19. We all have different experiences, so we each see things from a slightly different …… of view.
    A. stand    B. place    C. set    D. point

20. I find it difficult to put …… in my friend as he sometimes doesn't tell the truth.
    A. trust    B. confidence    C. belief    D. faith

21. Some university students hope to visit Europe because it has a long and …… history.
    A. wealthy    B. rich    C. poor    D. straight

22. Parents often try to help their children …… an interest in books by reading aloud to them.
    A. assist    B. distribute    C. develop    D. arrange

23. Having patience can help to avoid some problems caused by a language …….
    A. wall    B. barrier    C. block    D. net

24. A lot of a teacher's time is …… by preparing for classes and correcting examinations.
    A. slipped    B. solved    C. occupied    D. broken

25. A good relationship is one in which people treat each other with …….
    A. relate    B. regret    C. refer    D. respect

# Chapter 7  Questions about Canada (from Atsushi to Yumi)
## カナダの語学留学（バンクーバー）

パートⅡではパートⅠで登場した学生と新たに海外で学びたいという学生が、留学に関して話し合います。彼らの会話を通じて口語表現を学ぶとともに各国における留学事情に関して理解を深めていきます。

本章ではバンクーバーに3か月間滞在しているユミが、アツシの質問に答えます。

## I. Vocabulary Preview

本章で扱う語(句)です。それぞれの意味を表す日本語を選びなさい。

1. detailed ( )  2. institute ( )  3. require ( )
4. appropriate ( )  5. recommend ( )  6. preparation ( )

a. 依頼する　b. 要求する　c. 妥当な
d. 詳しい　e. （学校などの）機関　f. 推薦する
g. 準備

## II. Introduction

本章で扱う内容の紹介です。英文にさっと目を通して、次の問いに英語で答えなさい。　Track 26

Atsushi, a student at Yumi's university, is thinking of going to Canada to improve his English. His teacher, Mr. Smith, advises him to contact Yumi who is currently studying there. He wants to get detailed information about the timetable at the language center. He is also interested in what he will be expected to talk about in his classes in Canada.

(1) Why did Atsushi make contact with Yumi?

(2) Yumi and Atsushi are both Japanese. Why do you think they communicate with each other in English?

## III. Reading

ユミとアツシの会話です。読んで問いに答えなさい。

Track 27

**Atsushi:** Hello, Yumi! I'm going to Canada next year. Could you tell me something about the English classes at the language school you attend?

**Yumi:** Hi, Atsushi. It's great that you are thinking of coming to Canada! Well, classes at the English Language Institute usually start at 09:00. However, I arrive a little earlier as it **allows me to** chat with my friends before classes begin. We have a **timetable** of four hours of classes per day: two 90-minute English classes in the morning, then a 60-minute Canadian culture class in the afternoon after lunch. We also have some activities during the week.

**Atsushi:** Thanks Yumi. Please advise me about what **preparation** I should do before going to Canada.

**Yumi:** Well, I wish I had spent more time researching my own culture before coming over here, as it is **hard** for me to answer when asked about Japan and Japanese culture. I think you should study as much about Japan as possible before coming to Canada.

**Atsushi:** How about the level of English required? I'm worried as I often make mistakes when using English. Is there a class suitable for me at the school in Canada?

**Yumi:** This school does not have any particular **requirements**. Students take a placement test and are then placed into appropriate classes depending on their scores. Some schools require you to have a high score in an international test, such as the TOEFL or IELTS. Atsushi, how do you study English in Japan? I recommend that you find your own way to study, and not depend only on what is done in school.

**Atsushi:** Ok, I'll think about what I can do.

## 1. *Words & Phrases*

本文の太字の語句の中から適切なものを選んで空所に記入しなさい。

(1) Some people think learning to drive is easy, while others think it is (                    ).

(2) According to the bus (                    ), the next one comes at 11:30.

(3) Both skill and (                    ) are important to be successful.

(4) The (                    ) for studying abroad are a basic level of English and the courage to use it.

(5) My piano teacher (                    ) practice on her favorite piano.

## 2. *Grammar*
空所に適語を入れてそれぞれ 2 つの表現が同じような意味になるようにしなさい。

(1) A. I'm going to Canada next year. I'm getting ready for my journey at the moment.
　　B. I've decided to go to Canada next year. Now I'm (     ) for the trip.
　　① willing　　　　② traveling　　　　③ trying　　　　④ preparing

(2) A. My husband is (     ) about his job. It tires me out.
　　B. I am fed up with my husband saying that he is not happy with his job.
　　① always complaining　　② sometimes concerned
　　③ often thinking　　　　　④ never talking

## 3. *Understanding the Text*
次の質問に英語で答えなさい。

(1) Why does Yumi arrive earlier at her school in the morning?
　　It allows her to _____.

(2) What do the students in Yumi's school learn after lunch?
　　They learn _____.

(3) What does Yumi regret?
　　She regrets not _____.

(4) What is Atsushi worried about?
　　_____.

(5) How will the school in Canada place Atsushi in a suitable class?
　　_____.

Let's Get Out of Japan!

# IV. Listening

## 1. *Filling in the Blanks*

アツシが大学の国際交流センターのスミス先生と話しています。CD を聴いて各空所に 1 語を入れなさい。

Track 28
Track 29

### Atsushi and Mr. Smith's Conversation

| Part 1 | 1. Yumi's comment _____ Atsushi. |
| | 2. People often ask Mr. Smith about life in the _____. |
| | 3. Atsushi feels his life is not very _____. |
| Part 2 | 1. The people Atsushi meets will be _____ in the food he eats. |
| | 2. Atsushi decides to also talk about his _____. |
| | 3. Atsushi realises that he _____ to study about Japan. |

## 2. *Understanding the Dialog*

次は先ほどの会話の一部です。読んで、質問に答えなさい。

\*\*\*\*\*\*\*\*\*\*\*\*\*\*\*\*\*\*\*\*\*\*\*\*\*\*\*\*\*\*\*\*\*\*\*\*\*\*\*\*\*\*\*\*\*\*\*\*\*\*\*\*\*\*\*\*\*\*\*\*\*\*\*\*\*\*\*\*\*\*\*\*\*\*\*\*\*\*\*\*\*\*\*\*

**From PART 1:** What Surprised Atsushi?

**Mr. Smith:** *I've realized that when you travel abroad the people you meet are very interested in hearing about your life in your home country.*

**Atsushi:** *Yes, that makes sense.*

(1) What are people interested in hearing about, according to Mr. Smith?

_____.

\*\*\*\*\*\*\*\*\*\*\*\*\*\*\*\*\*\*\*\*\*\*\*\*\*\*\*\*\*\*\*\*\*\*\*\*\*\*\*\*\*\*\*\*\*\*\*\*\*\*\*\*\*\*\*\*\*\*\*\*\*\*\*\*\*\*\*\*\*\*\*\*\*\*\*\*\*\*\*\*\*\*\*\*

**From PART 2:** Things You May be Asked

**Mr. Smith:** *You may be asked some difficult questions, too, such as about the Japanese economy.*

**Atsushi:** *Yumi was right!*

(2) What difficult topic may Atsushi be asked about in Canada?

_____.

*Chapter 7 Questions about Canada (from Atsushi to Yumi)* 47

## Information Column: Maple Syrup

カナダの国旗は、赤い葉が中央に配置され、とても親しみやすいです。この葉はサトウカエデという種類の木の葉で、この木の樹液からメープルシロップが生成されます。"Nothing is more Canadian than maple syrup" と言われるほど、メープルシロップはカナダ人の生活に欠かせないものです。集めた樹液を煮詰めて甘味料をつくる方法は、北米に元々住んでいた先住民の知恵でした。ヨーロッパ人の入植者がその過程を改良し、今日の産業に発展したわけです。

## V. Collocations

1. 語と語のつながりに注目して空所に最も適切な語を入れなさい。

(1) Atsushi doesn't think his English is very good. In other words, he (     ) **confidence** in his English ability.
   ① misses  ② lacks  ③ slips  ④ fails
      E         O         A         I

(2) When Atsushi has a question about Canada, he knows he can (     ) **help** from Yumi. Of course, she is always glad to help him.
   ① seek  ② look  ③ find  ④ search
      D         H         P         C

(3) While there are many countries in which Atsushi can learn English, he is seriously (     ) **of going** to Canada.
   ① considering  ② concerning  ③ thinking  ④ deciding
          A                E                  O              U

(4) Yumi (     ) she had gained more **knowledge** about her own country before going abroad.
   ① hopes  ② expects  ③ worries  ④ wishes
      G           R            B            F

2. 各正解選択肢の下にある赤色ローマ字を組み合わせて空所に入る単語を作りなさい。

"Japanese (          ) such as sushi is famous all over the world."

48    Let's Get Out of Japan!

## 🌐 VI. Writing

下記はアツシのブログの一部です。日本語に合うように下記の英文の続きを、与えられた語句を組み合せて完成しなさい。ただし、<u>それぞれ1語を補い、文頭は大文字に直しなさい</u>。

> 両親と海外研修について話し合いました。一生懸命勉強する、と約束できるなら行ってもよいと言ってくれました。(1)ユミさんのアドバイスに従って、カナダに行くことに決めました。(2)出発する前に、日本と日本文化についても、もっと学びたい！

*I discussed the study abroad program with my parents. They said I could go if I promised to study hard.*

(1)　① decided to　② Yumi's advice　③ and go to Canada　④ I have

_____.

(2)　① I want to　② Japan and Japanese　③ learn more about　④ culture before

_____.

## 🌐 VII. What Can You Do Now?

最後に下記の3つの到達目標を読んで、できるものにチェックを入れなさい。

<u>*I can*</u>

☐ *describe a typical timetable at a language school.*

☐ *be prepared for what foreign people may ask me when I go abroad.*

☐ *improve my English skills even when I am with my Japanese friends.*

*Chapter 7 Questions about Canada (from Atsushi to Yumi)*

# Chapter 8  *Questions about Australia (from Mariko to Masaru)*
## オーストラリアの語学留学（パース）

本章ではオーストラリアで留学中のマサルが、本格的に留学を希望しているマリコの質問に答えます。

## I. Vocabulary Preview

本章で扱う語（句）です。それぞれの意味を表す日本語を選びなさい。

1. vast （　　） 2. appealing to （　　） 3. marsupial （　　）
4. deport （　　） 5. civilisation （　　） 6. survive （　　）

| | | |
|---|---|---|
| a. 国外追放する | b. 文明 | c. 広大な |
| d. 有袋類 | e. 輸入する | f. 生き残る |
| g. 興味をそそる | | |

## II. Introduction

本章で扱う内容の紹介です。英文にさっと目を通して、次の問いに英語で答えなさい。　　Track 30

> Mariko, a student at Masaru's university, would like to go to Australia not only to learn English but also to study other subjects as part of a regular university course. She is very interested in learning about Australian nature and history. Her teacher advises her to contact Masaru and ask him about his studies in Australia.

(1) Mariko would like to learn English in Australia. What else would she like to learn?

(2) What do you think Mariko can learn from Masaru?

## III. Reading

マリコとマサルの会話です。読んで問いに答えなさい。　　　　　　　　　　Track 31

**Mariko:** Hello, Masaru! I'm considering studying abroad in Australia next year. What are you studying?

**Masaru:** I'm studying English and I'm also taking four regular subjects: The Australian Economy, Australian Nature, Australian History, and Aboriginal Art.

**Mariko:** That sounds appealing to me. Could you tell me details of the classes, especially about Australian Nature and Australian History?

**Masaru:** We learned that Australia is a vast land with nature that developed separately from the other continents over millions of years. This produced a **flora and fauna** largely **unique to** Australia.

**Mariko:** Yes, marsupials are one example, isn't that right? They have a pouch which they use to **raise their young.** I'd like to see such animals with my own eyes.

**Masaru:** Then, as you know, Europeans arrived only several hundred years ago. Surprisingly, some of those early settlers were British people who had been forced to leave their own country due to having committed only **petty crimes**.

**Mariko:** Is that true? What kind of crimes do you mean?

**Masaru:** For example, if someone was hungry and stole some bread, they might have been deported in those days. The early settlers in Sydney included thousands of such people.

**Mariko:** How did they survive after they arrived in such a land untouched by Western civilisation?

**Masaru:** It was a struggle at first as everything had to be built **from scratch**. The Aborigines were already there, of course, but their way of life was different from that of Europeans.

**Mariko:** I'm looking forward to learning as much as you have, Masaru.

## 1. *Words & Phrases*

本文の太字の語句の中から適切なものを選んで空所に記入しなさい。

(1) I began to learn Russian this year. At the beginning, I didn't have any knowledge at all, so I had to start (　　　　　　　).

(2) (　　　　　　　), such as the act of people stealing an umbrella when it suddenly begins to rain, are not uncommon in Japan.

(3) While there is a huge number of planets in the universe, some scientists think that life is (　　　　　　　　) Planet Earth.

(4) The (　　　　　　　　) of the Galapagos Islands was so diverse that Darwin was inspired to write about them.

(5) Some birds such as swallows make their nests and (　　　　　　　　) in the entrances of buildings.

## 2. *Grammar*
空所に適語を入れてそれぞれ2つの表現が同じような意味になるようにしなさい。

(1) A. Some companies have their employees work extra for no reward.
　　B. Some companies (　　) their employees to work overtime without pay.
　　① let　　　　　　② make　　　　　　③ force　　　　　　④ insist

(2) A. After listening to my plan, my parents said they would let me study abroad.
　　B. My parents (　　) me to study abroad when I told them about my plan.
　　① told　　　　　② allowed　　　　　③ expected　　　　　④ hoped

## 3. *Understanding the Text*
次の質問に英語で答えなさい。

(1) What is Mariko considering doing?
　　She is considering _____.

(2) Apart from regular subjects, what is Masaru studying?
　　He is studying _____.

(3) In what way has Australian nature developed over a long period of time?
　　It has developed _____.

(4) What type of people did the early settlers in Sydney include?
　　_____.

(5) Were the Europeans the first people in Australia? If not, who were there before them?
　　_____.

# IV. Listening

## 1. *Filling in the Blanks*

マリコが、日本訪問中のオーストラリアからのルークと話しています。CD を聴いて各空所に1語を入れなさい。

Track 32
Track 33

### Mariko and Luke's Conversation

| Part 1 | 1. Mariko is going to Australia _____ summer. |
| --- | --- |
| | 2. Mariko would like to know how to _____ in Australia. |
| | 3. Laughing and telling _____ are important for Australians. |
| Part 2 | 1. Mariko asks Luke to _____ her list. |
| | 2. Luke notices that Mariko doesn't have swimming _____ on her list. |
| | 3. Luke says these are necessary to _____ Australian life. |

## 2. *Understanding the Dialog*

次は先ほどの会話の一部です。読んで、質問に答えなさい。

**From PART 1:** Advice from an Australian

**Mariko:** I'm going to Australia this summer.

**Luke** Do not spend too much time in the shower—water is a precious resource in Australia.

(1) Why shouldn't Mariko take a long shower in Australia?

_____.

**From PART 2:** Things You Need in Australia

**Mariko:** What kind of activities do Australians do at the seaside?

**Luke:** People of all ages enjoy various water sports, although surfing is done mainly by younger people.

(2) What kind of water sports is a young girl like Mariko likely to do?

_____.

*Chapter 8 Questions about Australia (from Mariko to Masaru)*

### Information Column: Flying Doctors and Education

オーストラリアには、シドニー、パース、メルボルンといった大きな都市がありますが、人口がまばらな地域が大半です。実際、隣人から数十キロも離れて暮らしている家族が多数あります。彼らが抱える大きな問題は、医療と教育へのアクセスです。医療に関して言えば、'flying doctor' システムが大いに役立っています。医師が飛行機に乗って往診する医療サービスで、広大な国土に暮らすうえで欠かせない社会システムです。

地理的に孤立して暮らす子供たちは、毎日学校に通うことはできません。オーストラリアではなんと 1918 年に 'SIDE' (School of Isolated and Distance Education) という制度ができました。1940 年代にはラジオで毎日、授業を配信したり、教師がはるばる車で各家庭に出向いたりしていました。現代ではインターネットを通じて生徒と先生が対話して授業を効果的に行っています。

## V. Collocations

**1.** 語と語のつながりに注目して空所に最も適切な語を入れなさい。

(1) Australian children are expected to help with housework. For example, they are often sent to the store to buy a (　　　) **of bread** or a carton of milk.

① bag　　　② box　　　③ loaf　　　④ barrel
　A　　　　　I　　　　　U　　　　　O

(2) Australians like eating fruit. You can find a (　　　) **of bananas or grapes** in the fruit basket in many houses.

① set　　　② bunch　　　③ collection　　　④ group
　N　　　　　T　　　　　　Y　　　　　　　　F

(3) Mariko prefers to write her essays by hand, rather than type them on a computer. Her essay about Australia was very long. She used twenty (　　　) **of paper**!

① slices　　② clusters　　③ sheets　　④ crowds
　I　　　　　A　　　　　　E　　　　　　O

(4) Masaru put up his umbrella after he felt a (　　　) **of rain** fall on his head.

① ball　　　② drop　　　③ piece　　　④ circle
　M　　　　　B　　　　　　C　　　　　　K

**2.** 各正解選択肢の下にある赤色ローマ字を組み合わせて空所に入る単語を作りなさい。

　Mariko bought a travel set which included deodorant, a toothbrush and a (　　　　) of toothpaste.

54　Let's Get Out of Japan!

# VI. Writing

下記はマリコのブログの一部です。日本語に合うように下記の英文の続きを、与えられた語句を組み合せて完成しなさい。ただし、それぞれ1語を補い、文頭は大文字に直しなさい。

> あと3か月足らずでオーストラリアに出発します。先生からは準備しなければならない物のリストを作るように、と言われています。⁽¹⁾まず第一にすべきことは、入国ビザを申請することです。⁽²⁾円をオーストラリアドルに両替しておくことも必要です。

*I will leave for Australia in less than three months' time. My teacher told me to make a list of things I need to prepare.*

(1)  ① do is to   ② the first   ③ thing I must   ④ for an immigration visa

_____.

(2)  ① Australian dollars   ② have to   ③ Japanese yen for   ④ I also

_____.

# VII. What Can You Do Now?

最後に下記の3つの到達目標を読んで、できるものにチェックを入れなさい。

*I can*

☐ *name some leisure activities Australians like to do by the sea.*

☐ *say something about the history of Australia.*

☐ *give an example of an educational system that overcomes the problems of geographic isolation.*

# Chapter 9   Questions about Britain (from Naomi to Kenta)
## イギリスの寮生活（エジンバラ）

この章ではスコットランドに滞在している
ケンタが、ナオミの質問に答えて、寮生活
のエピソードを話します。

## I. Vocabulary Preview

本章で扱う語（句）です。それぞれの意味を表す日本語を選びなさい。

1. nationality    (    )    2. dormitory    (    )    3. previous    (    )
4. in common    (    )    5. foreign    (    )    6. and so forth    (    )

| | | |
|---|---|---|
| a. 寮 | b. 共通の | c. 以前の |
| d. 国籍 | e. 〜など | f. 外国の |
| g. 又は | | |

## II. Introduction

本章で扱う内容の紹介です。英文にさっと目を通して、次の問いに英語で答えなさい。　　Track 34

　　Naomi, a student at Kenta's university, is interested in studying abroad. She is especially interested in going to an English speaking country in Europe. Her teacher advises her to contact Kenta who is currently studying in Scotland. Kenta stayed with the Brown family before moving to the university dormitory. However, Naomi doesn't know about that.

(1) Where in the world does Naomi want to study abroad?


(2) What questions do you think Naomi would like to ask him?

## III. Reading

ナオミとケンタの会話です。読んで問いに答えなさい。

Track 35

**Naomi:** Hello, Kenta! I would like to go to Europe. I heard you are studying in Scotland. How is your life there? Do you **get on well** with your home stay family?

**Kenta:** Life in Scotland really **suits me.** My home stay family were all wonderful, but now I'm staying in the university dormitory!

**Naomi:** Was there any particular reason you moved to the dormitory? Did you have any trouble with the home stay family?

**Kenta:** Not at all. They were great. Most regular students here stay in dormitories, so I also wanted to experience such a life. However, it took a while to **get used to.**

**Naomi:** So, what's it like?

**Kenta:** Five students live in the same unit. We each have our own room and bathroom, but we share the kitchen and living room. The nationalities of the students in my group are Brazilian, Mexican, British, Chinese, and Japanese, me. There were some problems at the beginning, **to be honest**. For example, we share a big fridge so we sometimes made a mistake by using other students' food. Also, the kitchen could be too crowded in the evenings.

**Naomi:** How did you **overcome such problems**?

**Kenta:** Talking about it together enabled us to solve the fridge problem. Also, we decided to take turns to cook dinner, so the kitchen is never crowded anymore. I cook for everyone on Tuesdays. I make Japanese food such as *nikujaga*, *yakisoba*, and *curry and rice*. I can relax on the other days, and try Chinese, Mexican, Brazilian, and British food. Then, we sometimes go to a restaurant together on weekends.

## 1. *Words & Phrases*

本文の太字の語句の中から適切なものを選んで空所に記入しなさい。

(1) I like bright colors. I have a yellow and light blue sweater that (　　　　　　) perfectly.

(2) Kenta enjoyed living with the Brown family but, (　　　　　　), he prefers living with people his own age.

(3) It can take a long time for study abroad students to (　　　　　　) the way of life in their host country.

(4) Life is not easy sometimes. Study may be difficult, it might be hard to find a job, etc. However, with hard work and a little luck, you can (                    ).

(5) My best friend and I (                    ) together. Maybe it is because we have similar interests.

## 2. *Grammar*
空所に適語を入れてそれぞれ2つの表現が同じような意味になるようにしなさい。

(1) A. My grandmother has decided to sleep in our house while the repair work on her house is going on.
B. My grandmother's house is being repaired, so she (    ) at my house until the work is finished.
　① had stayed　　② used to stay　　③ is staying　　④ has stayed

(2) A. I'm working in the sales department now, but I heard that I will move to a new department in a few weeks.
B. I (    ) to the sales department now, but I am going to be transferred to another department next month.
　① travel　　② attend　　③ join　　④ belong

## 3. *Understanding the Text*
次の質問に英語で答えなさい。

(1) Why did Kenta move out of the Brown family house and into the university dormitory?
He wanted to _____.

(2) How many people live with Kenta, and what are their nationalities?
Four people live _____.

(3) What two problems did Kenta mention when describing his dormitory life?
Some people made _____.

(4) They solved one problem by talking about it. How did they solve the other problem?
_____.

(5) If you were Kenta, what would you make for the other students for dinner?
_____.

# IV. Listening

## 1. Filling in the Blanks

ナオミは、来日中であるロンドン出身のデビッドとイギリス留学について話しています。CDを聴いて各空所に1語を入れなさい。

Track 36
Track 37

### Naomi and David's Conversation

| Part 1 | 1. Living in a dormitory with other students sounds _____. |
|---|---|
| | 2. Kenta's situation seems like a good _____ to learn. |
| | 3. Naomi will try to _____ her parents. |
| Part 2 | 1. David suggests that London _____ suit her. |
| | 2. If you catch the train to France, you will _____ in less than three hours. |
| | 3. Naomi thanks David for his _____ advice. |

## 2. Understanding the Dialog

次は先ほどの会話の一部です。読んで、質問に答えなさい。

*********************************************************************

**From PART 1:** An Opportunity to Learn

**Naomi:** *He is living in a dormitory with other students from various countries.*

**David:** *I'm sure they all speak to each other in English because it is the language of international communication.*

(1) Why is David sure that the students all speak together using English?

_____.

*********************************************************************

**From PART 2:** London is Convenient

**Naomi:** *How would London differ from Scotland as a place to study?*

**David:** *The quality of education is great in both places. However, it is easier to travel to many European countries from London.*

(2) What do London and Scotland have in common, according to David?

_____.

### Information Column: Red Hair in Scotland

　映画「ハリーポッター」に登場する主人公ハリーの親友であるロンは、ユーモラスな赤毛の男の子です。赤毛 (red hair) を持つ人は、世界の人口の 1 ～ 2%程度と推定されていますが、スコットランドでは全人口のなんと 13%近くが赤毛で、世界で最もその割合が多い地域です。少数派ゆえ、赤毛の人はヨーロッパ社会で長い間偏見や差別の対象となることがありました。赤毛は、幾分侮蔑的に 'ginger hair'、赤毛の人は 'redhead' と呼ばれることがあります。

　その表現を逆手にとって、2013 年 8 月スコットランドの中心都市エディンバラで、'Ginger Pride Walk' という赤毛の人々のパレードがありました。赤毛を持つ人々が、自分たちの特徴を誇りに思っていることを示すための行進で、大きな話題になりました。

## V. Collocations

**1.** 語と語のつながりに注目して空所に最も適切な語を入れなさい。

(1) Naomi is looking forward to going to Europe. She hopes she will be able to go on a **shopping** (　　　) in both Paris and London.
　① trip　　　② store　　　③ mall　　　④ fall
　　T　　　　　P　　　　　W　　　　　V

(2) Before Kenta left Japan for Britain, he bought a (　　　) **ticket** instead of a one-way ticket.
　① back　　　② return　　　③ repeat　　　④ double
　　O　　　　　U　　　　　I　　　　　A

(3) Kenta told Naomi that she can often get a **student** (　　　) if she shows her student identification card when she buys something.
　① bargain　　　② reduce　　　③ decrease　　　④ discount
　　Y　　　　　N　　　　　K　　　　　R

(4) In order to avoid (　　　) **your flight**, you should arrive at the airport at least two hours in advance.
　① miss　　　② missed　　　③ missing　　　④ will miss
　　E　　　　　U　　　　　O　　　　　A

**2.** 各正解選択肢の下にある赤色ローマ字を組み合わせて空所に入る単語を作りなさい。

'A good way to see a new city is to go on a bus (　　　　　)'.

## VI. Writing

下記はナオミのブログの一部です。日本語に合うように下記の英文の続きを、与えられた語句を組み合せて完成しなさい。ただし、それぞれ1語を補い、文頭は大文字に直しなさい。

> ケンタによると、スコットランドは英語を学ぶのに素晴らしい場所です。しかし、デビットと話したことでロンドンに行きたいという考えもわいてきました。(1) どちらにするかを決める為に、家族と友人にアドバイスを求めるつもりです。(2) 結論は何であろうと、留学することは私の人生をきっと豊かにするでしょう。

*According to Kenta, Scotland is a wonderful place to study English. However, speaking to my friend David put the idea of going to London in my mind.*

(1)　①to help me decide　②I'm going to ask　③friends for some　④my family and

_____.

(2)　①enrich my life　②I decide to　③will surely　④do, studying abroad

_____.

## VII. What Can You Do Now?

最後に下記の3つの到達目標を読んで、できるものにチェックを入れなさい。

*I can*

☐ *be prepared for some problems when staying in a student dormitory.*

☐ *understand how important English is in both private and business life.*

☐ *compare two places in Britain.*

*Chapter 9 Questions about Britain (from Naomi to Kenta)*

# Chapter 10　Questions about Singapore (from Satoko to Miki)
### シンガポールのインターンシップ（シンガポール）

本章ではシンガポールでインターンシップを体験したミキが、大学１年生のサトコの質問に答えます。

## I. Vocabulary Preview

本章で扱う語（句）です。それぞれの意味を表す日本語を選びなさい。

1. fluent (　　)　2. transfer (　　)　3. academic achievements (　　)
4. job seekers (　　)　5. qualification (　　)　6. personality (　　)

> a. 学業成績　b. 転勤させる　c. 就職希望者
> d. 採用通知　e. 流暢な　f. 資格
> g. 人格

## II. Introduction

本章で扱う内容の紹介です。英文にさっと目を通して、次の問いに英語で答えなさい。　　Track 38

> Satoko, a first year university student, is fluent in English. She lived in the USA for three years when she was a child because her father was transferred there. Satoko is very eager to learn about Miki's time in Singapore as Miki stayed there previously on a working holiday.

(1) Why is Satoko fluent in English?

(2) Satoko is interested in working abroad. How about you? Would you like to work abroad in the future? Why/Why not?

## III. Reading

サトコとミキの会話です。読んで問いに答えなさい。

Track 39

**Satoko:** Hello, Miki! I heard you worked in Singapore for six months. I'd love to hear all about your time there!
**Miki:** Sure, Satoko. These days, many Japanese people visit Singapore for both business and pleasure. Tourists can stay without any visa, but if you want to work there, it's a **completely different matter**.
**Satoko:** I'd like to know about working in Singapore as I plan to work there in the future. Could you please give me a **piece of advice**?
**Miki:** Well, the Singapore government welcomes workers from other countries. **Job seekers** first need to apply for a visa matching the work they plan to do. The government strictly examines the applications and, based on each applicant's skills and qualifications, decides whether or not to issue a visa.
**Satoko:** What skills do job seekers need?
**Miki:** It depends on your purpose. For example, if you hope to work as an engineer, you need to show your high academic achievements and excellent work experience. If you want to enter Singapore as an entrepreneur, you have to show your original ideas and detailed business plans.
**Satoko:** The ability to speak English is essential in Singapore, isn't it?
**Miki:** That's right. You also need to have good business skills and a strong **work ethic**. Just having good grades in school or university is not enough. The manager in my company told me that it is important to be a **self-starter**, yet be able to work as part of a team.
**Satoko:** I think that developing a balanced personality is required in business in every country in the world.

## 1. *Words & Phrases*

本文の太字の語句の中から適切なものを選んで空所に記入しなさい。

(1) I love baking so I opened a cake shop. However, making a profit was a
 (                    ), so I ended up having to close it down.

(2) My father gave me an important (                    ) when I was a child. He told me to always tell the truth.

(3) I think I am more intelligent than my brother. However, because of his
 (                    ), he is more successful than I am.

(4) My elder brother is a (                    ). He never waits for someone to tell him what work to do.

(5) Interviewers are happy when (                    ) have skills that the company needs.

## 2. *Grammar*
空所に適語を入れてそれぞれ 2 つの表現が同じような意味になるようにしなさい。

(1) A. You need a lot of experience in order to make a good presentation in English.
　　B. (　　) a good presentation in English requires a lot of experience.
　　① Make　　　　② Making　　　　③ The making　　④ How to make

(2) A. The old man told me that he was pleased to meet me at the party.
　　B. The old man at the party said to me, 'It is/was a pleasure (　　) you'.
　　① meeting　　　② with meeting　　③ meet　　　　④ of meeting

## 3. *Understanding the Text*
次の質問に英語で答えなさい。

(1) According to Miki, for what purpose do Japanese people visit Singapore?
　　They visit Singapore for both _____.

(2) What type of people need a visa to stay in Singapore?
　　People who want to _____.

(3) Why does Satoko ask Miki for advice?
　　(She does so) because she wants to _____.

(4) What else do entrepreneurs need to show besides detailed business plans?
　　_____.

(5) What kind of personality does Satoko think is important to develop?
　　_____.

## IV. Listening

### 1. *Filling in the Blanks*

サトコがアドバイザー（村上ジョンさん /Mr John Murakami）と話しています。CD を聴いて各空所に 1 語を入れなさい。

Track 40
Track 41

#### Satoko and Mr Murakami's Conversation

| Part 1 | 1. Satoko _____ to Miki about Singapore. |
| --- | --- |
| | 2. Singapore also accepts other_____ of job seekers. |
| | 3. Housemaids come from _____ countries. |
| Part 2 | 1. _____ to a TV program, there are a lot of Japanese restaurants in Singapore. |
| | 2. The number of restaurants is still _____. |
| | 3. Japanese _____ and local people in Singapore enjoy Japanese food. |

### 2. *Understanding the Dialog*

次は先ほどの会話の一部です。読んで、質問に答えなさい。

\*\*\*\*\*\*\*\*\*\*\*\*\*\*\*\*\*\*\*\*\*\*\*\*\*\*\*\*\*\*\*\*\*\*\*\*\*\*\*\*\*\*\*\*\*\*\*\*\*\*\*\*\*\*\*\*\*\*\*\*\*\*\*\*\*\*\*\*\*\*\*\*\*\*\*\*\*\*\*\*

**From PART 1:** Jobs Available in Singapore

**Satoko:** *The Singapore government welcomes foreign workers.*

**Mr Murakami:** *That's right. The government knows that inviting innovative business people and engineers to Singapore benefits the economy.*

(1) What kind of foreign workers benefit the economy in Singapore?

_____.

\*\*\*\*\*\*\*\*\*\*\*\*\*\*\*\*\*\*\*\*\*\*\*\*\*\*\*\*\*\*\*\*\*\*\*\*\*\*\*\*\*\*\*\*\*\*\*\*\*\*\*\*\*\*\*\*\*\*\*\*\*\*\*\*\*\*\*\*\*\*\*\*\*\*\*\*\*\*\*\*

**From PART 2:** Japanese Entrepreneurs

**Satoko:** *Miki said to me she often came across new ramen restaurants when she went shopping.*

**Mr Murakami:** *The program featured an ambitious young man who left Japan to start such a restaurant in Singapore.*

(2) What did the ambitious young man leave Japan to do?

_____.

*Chapter 10 Questions about Singapore (from Satoko to Miki)* 65

### Information Column: Singapore … the Place to Be

'If you were smart in 1807 you moved to London, if you were smart in 1907 you moved to New York City, and if you are smart in 2007 you move to Asia'. これは、アメリカ人投資家のジム・ロジャーズ氏の言葉です。現代におけるシンガポールの経済的成功と教育水準の高さを語るときにしばしば引用されます。ロジャーズ氏は家族を連れてシンガポールに移住し、娘を地元の有名校に通わせて中国語を学ばせました。シンガポールは、マレー語、中国語、英語、タミール語の４つを公用語に指定するとともに、小学校から積極的に英語教育に取り組み、近年は中国語教育にも力を入れ始めています。その一方で、街の屋台では、イギリス英語に他の言語表現が混じった 'Singlish' と呼ばれるやや癖のある英語や標準中国語に中国南部地方の方言が混じった中国語も聞かれます。

## V. Collocations

1. 語と語のつながりに注目して空所に最も適切な語を入れなさい。

(1) Satoko wants to (　　　) **a diary** when she goes abroad to remind her of her adventures.
　① make　　　　② hold　　　　③ save　　　　④ keep
　　W　　　　　　　E　　　　　　　H　　　　　　　T

(2) Many Singaporeans are multilingual, helping them (　　　) **to** various social and working situations.
　① change　　　② adapt　　　　③ fix　　　　④ swap
　　D　　　　　　　S　　　　　　　P　　　　　　　C

(3) Mr Murakami gave Satoko a book about the rules in Singapore because he didn't want her to find herself (　　　) **the law**.
　① snapping　　② cutting　　　③ breaking　　④ smashing
　　A　　　　　　　E　　　　　　　O　　　　　　　U

(4) Satoko would like to **work** (　　　) in the future.
　① global　　　② international　③ abroad　　　④ foreign
　　G　　　　　　　R　　　　　　　P　　　　　　　B

2. 各正解選択肢の下にある赤色ローマ字を組み合わせて空所に入る単語を作りなさい。

'When flying from Japan to Australia, you sometimes have to (　　　　　) over in Singapore for a few hours'.

Let's Get Out of Japan!

## VI. Writing

下記はサトコのブログの一部です。日本語に合うように下記の英文の続きを、与えられた語句を組み合せて完成しなさい。ただし、それぞれ1語を補い、文頭は大文字に直しなさい。

> ミキがシンガポールで過ごしていたときの話で盛り上がりました。素晴らしい経験でしたが、そこでは日本の物がなくて不自由したと言っていました。⑴日本の製品は手に入るけれども、選択の幅が限られていました。⑵それで、ミキのお母さんは彼女のお気に入りの化粧品をしばしば郵送しました。

*I enjoyed speaking with Miki about her time in Singapore. She said she had a wonderful experience there but she also missed some Japanese things.*

(1)　① buy Japanese　② was limited　③ goods there, the　④ although she could

_____.

(2)　① by post　② Miki her favourite　③ therefore, her　④ mother often sent

_____.

## VII. What Can You Do Now?

最後に下記の3つの到達目標を読んで、できるものにチェックを入れなさい。

*I can*

☐ *list some skills needed to enter Singapore.*

☐ *understand what opportunities there are for people who move to Singapore.*

☐ *talk about the languages taught and spoken in Singapore.*

*Chapter 10 Questions about Singapore (from Satoko to Miki)*

# Chapter 11  Questions about Ireland (from Shinichi to Maria)
## アイルランドの観光（ダブリン）

本章ではアイルランド（共和国）に滞在しているマリアが、シンイチの質問に答えます。

## I. Vocabulary Preview

本章で扱う語(句)です。それぞれの意味を表す日本語を選びなさい。

1. vicinity  (　　)　2. convert  (　　)　3. born and raised  (　　)
4. tranquil  (　　)　5. hot spot  (　　)　6. monument  (　　)

| | | |
|---|---|---|
| a. 遺跡 | b. （環境などに）落ち着く | c. 生まれ育つ |
| d. 人気のある場所 | e. 静かな | f. 改築する |
| g. 付近 | | |

## II. Introduction

本章で扱う内容の紹介です。英文にさっと目を通して、次の問いに英語で答えなさい。　　Track 42

> Shinichi is a student studying tourism at Maria's university. He has chosen to learn English in Ireland because it is a popular tourist destination with beautiful natural scenery, historic sites and buildings, and friendly and humorous people. He hopes to learn as much about tourism as he can while in Ireland, while also improving his English speaking skills. Shinichi meets Maria and asks her many questions.

(1) What is attractive about Ireland as a tourist destination?

(2) What questions do you think Shinichi would like to ask her?

## III. Reading

マリアとシンイチの会話です。読んで問いに答えなさい。　　　　　　　　　　Track 43

**Shinichi:** Maria, I'd like to visit some tourist spots this weekend. Where do you recommend?

**Maria:** Well, **in this vicinity**, there are lots of tranquil parks and relaxing walks along the riverside.

**Shinichi:** Great. How about some tourist **hot spots**?

**Maria:** There is a huge monument called 'Newgrange', a little outside Dublin. It is over 5,000 years old, so it is older than the pyramids in Egypt. I also recommend you to travel to other parts of Ireland to see the impressive castles and wonderful scenery there.

**Shinichi:** How long does it take?

**Maria:** Ireland is not a big country, so you can travel almost anywhere in a few hours from here. If I were you, I would spend time going around each of the four provinces.

**Shinichi:** Can you tell me a little more about them?

**Maria:** From a long time ago, Ireland has been divided into four parts. Each part has its own unique customs, clothing and food.

**Shinichi:** That sounds very interesting! What else do you recommend?

**Maria:** When you travel, you should stay in a **B&B** — that means 'Bed and Breakfast'. You can stay, at a reasonable price, in a local person's home which they have **converted** into a small hotel. All rooms have their own bathrooms. In the morning, you are served a delicious breakfast cooked by the owner of the house. A B&B is a great place to stay if you would like information about the local area, as the owner was usually **born and raised** there.

**Shinichi:** That's wonderful advice, Maria. Thank you!

## 1. *Words & Phrases*

本文の太字の語句の中から適切なものを選んで空所に記入しなさい。

(1) Tourist (　　　　　　　　　　) in Kyoto include Kiyomizu Temple and the Gion district.

(2) The delicious breakfast at the (　　　　　　　　　　) I stayed at was made using local ingredients.

(3) My parents (　　　　　　　　　　) our garage into a study for me. Now I can concentrate on my work.

(4) People who were (　　　　　　　　) in a certain town often know a lot about its history.

(5) Excuse me, do you know if there is a convenience store (　　　　　　　　)?

## 2. *Grammar*
空所に適語を入れてそれぞれ 2 つの表現が同じような意味になるようにしなさい。

(1) A. I hope my hotel room has been cleaned properly. I don't like dirty rooms.
　　B. I like clean hotel rooms. I wonder if my room (　　　).
　　① cleaned　　② is clean　　③ cleaning　　④ cleaner

(2) A. In Ireland, children learn Irish traditions from their parents. This way of teaching began a long time ago.
　　B. From a long time ago, Irish traditions (　　　) down from generation to generation.
　　① have been handed　② some hands　③ to hand　④ will be handed

## 3. *Understanding the Text*
次の質問に英語で答えなさい。

(1) Where does Maria recommend in the nearby area?
　　She recommended the _____.

(2) What can be found just outside Dublin?
　　You can find a _____.

(3) Why does Maria recommend Shinichi to go around each province?
　　Because each has _____.

(4) For what reasons does Maria recommend a B&B?
　　_____.

(5) Why does the owner of a B&B often have local information?
　　_____.

Let's Get Out of Japan!

## IV. Listening

### 1. *Filling in the Blanks*

シンイチがホームステイ先のお母さん（ケリー氏）と話しています。CD を聴いて各空所に1語を入れなさい。

Track 44
Track 45

**Shinichi and Mrs Kelly's Conversation**

| Part 1 | 1. There are five _____ people in Ireland.<br>2. Ireland has a small _____.<br>3. Shinichi often sees _____ of sightseers on his way back from school. |
|---|---|
| Part 2 | 1. The number of tourists is _____ than the population.<br>2. The large number of tourists helps the _____.<br>3. People in Ireland can find _____ in the tourism industry. |

### 2. *Understanding the Dialog*

次は先ほどの会話の一部です。読んで、質問に答えなさい。

**************************************************************************

**From PART 1:** A Popular Tourist Destination

**Shinichi:** *Ireland certainly seems to be a popular tourist destination.*

**Mrs Kelly:** *That's right. Actually, over six million tourists come to Ireland every year.*

(1) What information shows that Ireland is a popular tourist destination?

_____.

**************************************************************************

**From PART 2:** The Importance of Tourism

**Mrs Kelly:** *Many people in Ireland can find jobs in the tourism industry.*

**Shinichi:** *I want to learn as much as I can about tourism in Ireland. Then, I will bring that knowledge back to Japan.*

(2) What does Shinichi plan to do with the knowledge he gains?

_____.

### Information Column: Ireland Awaits

　首都ダブリンは、古い歴史と現代文化が混在する活気あふれる国際都市。ビジネス関係者はもちろん、世界各国から訪れる観光客や留学生でにぎわっています。一方、街を少し離れると緑豊かな土地が広がり、美しい自然の風景や息を飲むような景観に出会うことができます。また、古代の遺跡、ケルト文化の名残、中世の古城が各地に点在しています。

　アイルランド語には訪問者を 'one hundred thousand welcomes'（大歓迎）すると言う意味の言葉があるように、人々はおおらかで温かく迎え入れてくれます。アイルランド人の人柄や生活ぶりは、'There are two kinds of people in the world, the Irish and those who wish they were'.（世界には2種類の人々が住んでいます：アイルランド人と、アイルランド人になりたがっている人）という言葉でよく示されています。

## V. Collocations

**1. 語と語のつながりに注目して空所に最も適切な語を入れなさい。**

(1) Shinichi (　　　) **his bed** every morning before leaving for school.

① sets　　　② lays　　　③ makes　　　④ settles
　O　　　　　　E　　　　　　I　　　　　　　A

(2) After he graduates from university, Shinichi plans to (　　　) **for a job** in the tourism industry.

① rummage　　② find　　　③ seek　　　④ look
　F　　　　　　　B　　　　　L　　　　　　R

(3) One day, Maria (　　　) **a headache** so she couldn't go to school.

① had　　　② felt　　　③ did　　　④ hurt
　D　　　　　K　　　　　Y　　　　　W

(4) Japanese sizes and Irish sizes are different, so you should always (　　　) **clothes or shoes** before you buy them.

① try on　　② test on　　③ wear on　　④ place on
　E　　　　　U　　　　　　A　　　　　　I

**2. 各正解選択肢の下にある赤色ローマ字を組み合わせて空所に入る単語を作りなさい。**

Shinichi hopes to (　　　　　) a horse while he is in Ireland.

## VI. Writing

下記はシンイチのブログの一部です。日本語に合うように下記の英文の続きを、与えられた語句を組み合わせて完成しなさい。ただし、それぞれ1語を補い、文頭は大文字に直しなさい。

> 受け入れ先の家族が私をアイルランド南部への旅行に連れて行ってくれます。広々とした緑豊かな田園でハイキングをします。(1) そのあと、フェリーに乗って海岸沖の島々に行きます。(2) ホストファザーが釣りの仕方を教えると言ってくれました。

*My host family will take me on a trip to the south of Ireland. We will go hiking in the green and spacious countryside.*

(1)　① the coast　② catch a ferry　③ to some islands　④ then, we will

_____.

(2)　① would teach me　② my host father　③ how to　④ told me he

_____.

## VII. What Can You Do Now?

最後に下記の3つの到達目標を読んで、できるものにチェックを入れなさい。

*I can*

☐ *talk about some of the appealing points of Ireland.*

☐ *explain some benefits of staying in a B&B.*

☐ *point out how tourists can help the economy of a country.*

# Review Test II
## Chapters 7-11

*Choose the most suitable word or phrase for each blank space.*

1. A lot of staff resigned because they were …… with the complaints of their boss.
   - A. fed up
   - B. fed in
   - C. fed down
   - D. fed out

2. As children grow up, they …… their parents less and less until they finally become independent.
   - A. depend in
   - B. depend with
   - C. depend on
   - D. depend them

3. When elderly people become unable to take care of themselves, they often seek help …… their relatives or friends.
   - A. for
   - B. to
   - C. with
   - D. from

4. Art enthusiasts can spend hours …… at just one piece of art without becoming tired of it.
   - A. looking
   - B. look
   - C. looked
   - D. looker

5. I regret not …… my father's advice when he told me to follow my dream and take a chance in life.
   - A. taking
   - B. placing
   - C. adopting
   - D. permitting

6. Thanks to the Internet, …… education has become more popular and easier to take part in.
   - A. expanse
   - B. remote
   - C. far
   - D. distance

7. My friend's story about her home stay experience …… me to aim to go abroad myself.
   - A. inspired
   - B. investigated
   - C. instigated
   - D. inserted

8. A country's most precious …… is not oil or gas, it is the people living there.
   - A. material
   - B. fuel
   - C. resource
   - D. infrastructure

9. Not everyone living in big cities was born there. Some people moved in from …… areas.
   - A. rural
   - B. rustic
   - C. urban
   - D. metropolitan

10. Japanese cuisine is no longer …… Japan. Nowadays, it can be enjoyed all over the world.
    - A. unique for
    - B. unique to
    - C. unique in
    - D. unique with

11. When you start a new job in a new city, your …… is often either subsidized or provided by your company.
    - A. placement
    - B. accommodation
    - C. lifestyle
    - D. settlement

12. Being flexible can help you to understand and …… to a new culture.
    - A. take used
    - B. get used
    - C. take use
    - D. get use

13. My teacher gave me some …… advice on how to study, such as studying with a friend and setting realistic goals.

    A. improbable    B. probable    C. impractical    D. practical

14. Showing your student ID card entitles you to a …… at many stores.

    A. refund    B. bargain    C. discount    D. registration

15. Many companies …… employees to different cities or countries, allowing them to gain experience of a new place.

    A. remove    B. transfer    C. exchange    D. insert

16. People who are …… multiple languages often find it easier to get a job than those who are not.

    A. skilled in    B. skilled with    C. skilled for    D. skilled of

17. I don't like watching movies, but reading books is a completely different …….

    A. matter    B. substance    C. ingredient    D. element

18. Countries decide whether or not to …… a visa to visitors based on various criteria.

    A. send    B. issue    C. print    D. stamp

19. Companies like to hire people who are …… because they do a good job and need little supervision.

    A. regular workers    B. many skills    C. self-starters    D. freeze-dried

20. It is claimed that technology …… companies by allowing work to be done more efficiently, increasing productivity.

    A. benefits    B. profits    C. increases    D. constructs

21. Although John is handsome, clever and rich, his most …… point is his kindness.

    A. charm    B. appealing    C. raising    D. high

22. Fresh milk can be …… into cream, yogurt, cheese, and other dairy products.

    A. converted    B. mixed    C. altered    D. renovated

23. Some rich people go shopping in fashion …… such as Milan or Paris, where they can find the latest designs.

    A. cold places    B. cool areas    C. warm dots    D. hot spots

24. I'm planning to take my parents ……abroad after they retire to thank them for everything they have done for me.

    A. on a trip    B. in a holiday    C. over a journey    D. along an excursion

25. Every prefecture in Japan is different. You can find unique …… in almost every place you visit.

    A. duties    B. customs    C. civilizations    D. tolls

# Chapter 12   Applying for an Internship Program in Washington D.C.
## アメリカ合衆国のインターンシップ面接（ワシントン D.C.）

パートⅢでは英語を身に付けた学生が、学んだことを活かして、世界の各地に出かけます。シオリは芸術と言語を学んでいる大学2年生です。以前、家族と海外旅行を経験したことがありますが、今回は1人で出かけます。彼女は同じ大学に所属するカズからワシントンD.C.のインターンシップ・プログラムについて聞きました。

## I. Vocabulary Preview

本章で扱う語（句）です。それぞれの意味を表す日本語を選びなさい。

1. application form  (    )   2. exceed         (    )   3. determined   (    )
4. realize           (    )   5. enthusiastic   (    )   6. competitive  (    )

> a. 競争的な   b. 決意している   c. 設定する
> d. 実現する   e. 超える         f. 熱意のある
> g. 申請用紙

## II. Introduction

本章で扱う内容の紹介です。英文にさっと目を通して、次の問いに英語で答えなさい。　　Track 46

> Getting accepted to an internship program can be very competitive. Sometimes, the number of people who apply greatly exceed the number of jobs available. Therefore, you need to prepare well.
> 　In this chapter, a student, Shiori, tries to be accepted to a summer internship program in Washington D.C. She is determined to realize her dream of working in the USA.

(1) Why are some internship programs difficult to enter?


(2) What documents do you need to apply for an internship program, do you think?

## III. Reading

ワシントン D.C. には、市内の様々な博物館にインターンシップを希望する学生を送る機関があります。シオリはその組織の代表者と面接します。読んで問いに答えなさい。

Track 47

> **Manager:** Hello Shiori. I understand from your application form that you are **eager to** work at a museum in Washington D.C. Why is that?
>
> **Shiori:** Well, I am studying art and languages at university. I believe that the experience of working in a museum in the USA would **deepen my knowledge** about art and allow me to use my language skills.
>
> **Manager:** You spoke about how you would benefit from doing an internship. **On the other hand,** what would the museum gain from employing you?
>
> **Shiori:** I can speak English and Japanese, **enabling me to** work in both languages. I heard that many Japanese people visit museums in Washington D.C. so, for example, I would be able to help in guiding such people.
>
> **Manager:** I see. We are looking for someone with a wide range of knowledge. There is much more than art in a typical museum in Washington D.C. What are your feelings about that?
>
> **Shiori:** Yes, I have done research on the museums in the city, and found out that exhibits include **anything from** dinosaurs **to** space technology. For me, experiencing those things would be a vital part of my education. Such knowledge would give me a new perspective on the world. Also, I'm sure that my artistic background would help me to see things in a different way than some other people. This could allow me to explain things to visitors in a unique way.
>
> **Manager:** Good answer! I can feel that you are enthusiastic.
>
> **Shiori:** I hope you let me have the chance to show you just how enthusiastic I really am!

### 1. Words & Phrases

本文の太字の語句の中から適切なものを選んで空所に記入しなさい。

(1) Asking the teacher questions can (　　　　　　) about what I learn in class.

(2) My friend studies English hard as she is (　　　　　　) get a good score on her test.

(3) My grandmother always makes us a healthy breakfast, (　　　　　　) make a good start every morning.

*Chapter 12 Applying for an Internship Program in Washington D.C.*

(4) A manager's work can include (　　　　　　　　) dealing with customers to buying materials.

(5) Doing an internship can teach you important skills. (　　　　　　　　) it can be a waste of time if you do not work diligently.

## 2. *Grammar*
空所に適語を入れてそれぞれ 2 つの表現が同じような意味になるようにしなさい。

(1) A. I believe that anyone can be successful if they work hard.
　　B. (　　) that anyone can succeed provided they are serious about working.
　　① I'm afraid　　② I'm sure　　③ I'm proud　　④ I'm sorry

(2) A. I was afraid that the typhoon would hit our city.
　　B. I (　　) that the typhoon would pass over our city.
　　① was confused　　② was attracted　　③ was amazed　　④ was worried

## 3. *Understanding the Text*
次の質問に英語で答えなさい。

(1) How did the manager know that Shiori was eager to work at a museum?
　　He knew that because he read _____.

(2) What would the museum gain from employing Shiori?
　　She speaks Japanese so she would be able to _____.

(3) What type of person is the manager looking for?
　　He is looking for someone _____.

(4) How did Shiori find out that exhibits include anything from dinosaurs to space technology?
　　_____.

(5) What does the manager think about Shiori's last answer?
　　_____.

## IV. Listening

### 1. *Filling in the Blanks*

シオリが先輩のカズと話しています。CD を聴いて各空所に 1 語を入れなさい。

Track 48
Track 49

#### Shiori and Kazu's Conversation

| Part 1 | 1. Shiori was _____ at the interview. |
| --- | --- |
| | 2. Shiori hopes she will be _____. |
| | 3. Her email will show she is enthusiastic and _____. |
| Part 2 | 1. Shiori asks Kazu for some _____. |
| | 2. Kazu teaches Shiori a new English _____. |
| | 3. Shiori should _____ the rules of that place. |

### 2. *Understanding the Dialog*

次は先ほどの会話の一部です。読んで、質問に答えなさい。

*********************************************************************

**From PART 1:** Post-Interview Email

**Kazu:** *After the interview, did you send an email to the manager to say "thank you" for interviewing you?*

**Shiori:** *Yes, I did. I thought it would help to make a good impression.*

(1) What did Shiori think would help to make a good impression?

_____.

*********************************************************************

**From PART 2:** Advice from Kazu

**Shiori:** *Do you have any advice for me about working in Washington D.C.?*

**Kazu:** *When you go to the museum for the first time, you should observe other staff members and then try to behave like they do.*

(2) What does Kazu recommend Shiori do after observing other staff members?

_____.

*Chapter 12 Applying for an Internship Program in Washington D.C.*

## Information Column: The Smithsonian Institution

　ワシントン D.C. にあるスミソニアン協会は 19 の博物館・美術館といくつかの研究施設をもつ組織です。そのほか、付属の動物園もあります。例えば、国立自然史博物館に行けば、様々な古代生物の化石を見ることができます。また、国立航空宇宙博物館では、月の石に触れることができます。毎年およそ 3 千万人の人々が世界中から訪れますが、特別展示を除いては入場料は無料です。1 億 5 千万点近い展示物に加えて、ショップやレストランが充実しており、子供のためのスペースや多数の言語で利用できるガイドサービスも用意されています。ネットでも興味深い情報が絶えず発信されており、興味が尽きないサイト (www.si.edu) です。

## V. Collocations

1. 語と語のつながりに注目して空所に最も適切な語を入れなさい。

(1) The **best** (　　　) to visit old buildings is at night when they are lit up and there are fewer people around.
　① time　　　② day　　　③ hour　　　④ watch
　　W　　　　　W　　　　　A　　　　　U

(2) You usually have to (　　　) **an interview** before you are offered a job.
　① receive　　② conduct　　③ attend　　④ want
　　S　　　　　Q　　　　　K　　　　　M

(3) Although some Japanese museums are small, many have a (　　　) **collection** of items on display.
　① tiny　　　② fine　　　③ shabby　　④ shelf
　　A　　　　　O　　　　　E　　　　　I

(4) Shiori believes she will get a lot of **job** (　　　) from her work abroad.
　① pleasure　② delight　　③ satisfaction　④ happiness
　　G　　　　　B　　　　　R　　　　　H

2. 各正解選択肢の下にある赤色ローマ字を組み合わせて空所に入る単語を作りなさい。

　"Out of (　　　　　)"

Let's Get Out of Japan!

## VI. Writing

下記はシオリのブログの一部です。日本語に合うように下記の英文の続きを、与えられた語句を組み合せて完成しなさい。ただし、それぞれ1語を補い、文頭は大文字に直しなさい。

> 今日、カズが海外で暮らすことに関してアドバイスをしてくれました。地元の人と同じように生活するようにと教えてくれました。(1) しかし、自分の文化を重んじるべきであると父はいつも言っています。(2) やはり、その2つの意見の間でバランスをとるべきだと思います。

*Today, Kazu gave me advice about living abroad. He told me that I should live my life like the locals do.*

(1) ① always says that　② I should　③ however, my father　④ my own culture

_____.

(2) ① I think that　② I must　③ between both opinions　④ find a

_____.

## VII. What Can You Do Now?

最後に下記の3つの到達目標を読んで、できるものにチェックを入れなさい。

*I can*

☐ *say some questions that could be asked in an interview.*

☐ *talk about a way to make a good impression after an interview.*

☐ *name some things to do at the Smithsonian Institution in Washington D.C.*

# Chapter 13  University and Dormitory Life in Sweden
## スウェーデンの科目留学と学生寮生活（ストックホルム）

大学3年生のユウトが、スウェーデンに留学して、大学の寮に泊まります。英語が第二言語である環境でどのような生活が待っているのでしょうか。

## I. Vocabulary Preview

本章で扱う語（句）です。それぞれの意味を表す日本語を選びなさい。

1. efficient (　　) 2. exhausted (　　) 3. rubbish (　　)
4. subdivide (　　) 5. landfill (　　) 6. figure out (　　)

- a. 疲れ果てた
- b. 埋め立て地
- c. 効率的
- d. 把握する
- e. さらに分別する
- f. ゴミ
- g. 効果的

## II. Introduction

本章で扱う内容の紹介です。英文にさっと目を通して、次の問いに英語で答えなさい。

Track 50

　Yuto, a junior at university, has chosen to study abroad in Sweden to take classes in his university major, childhood studies.
　In this chapter, you will learn about Swedish society and culture including something about how Swedish people enjoy doing volunteer work. Although Swedish people speak Swedish as their native language, most of them can also communicate in English very well. In fact, many university courses in Sweden are taught through the English language.

(1) What will Yuto study in Sweden?


(2) At least how many languages can most people speak in Sweden?

## III. Reading

ユウトのメールを読んで問いに答えなさい。

Track 51

I arrived in Stockholm, the capital of Sweden and **made my way** to the university by bus. The **transport system** here is efficient, not unlike the Japanese system. On my arrival, I was met by some students who greeted me warmly and **showed me around** the university before bringing me to the university dormitory. I was completely exhausted by then, so I slept deeply.

The next day, I woke up and ate breakfast with other students in the shared kitchen. It was there that I had my first experience of **culture shock**. The nine rubbish bins in the kitchen really confused me as I couldn't figure out where to put my rubbish. I realised that rubbish isn't just divided, it's subdivided! Sara, another student in the dormitory, explained that this makes recycling easier, and that most cities divide rubbish into nine or ten categories. I thought that Swedish people have a positive attitude towards protecting the environment. They try to neither disturb nature nor waste resources and, in some towns, only 1% of waste goes to landfill.

I am **getting on well** at university. I am studying childhood studies as I want to work with children after graduating. It is amazing that, although most of the students here are Swedish, all our classes are taught in English. The high English ability of the Swedish people makes it easier for foreigners like me to live here without having to learn the local language. Tomorrow's class is about volunteer work. I'm looking forward to it!

## 1. *Words & Phrases*

本文の太字の語句の中から適切なものを選んで空所に記入しなさい。

(1) Japan has an efficient (　　　　　) which carries millions of people from place to place daily.

(2) People who travel to other countries can experience (　　　　　) when they come across things that are not usually found in their own country.

(3) 'Your boyfriend seems really nice, Julie'.
'Thank you. We are really (　　　　　) with each other. I hope we will get married some day'!

(4) I didn't have enough money for the bus so I (　　　　　) home on foot. I had to walk for one hour!

Chapter 13 University and Dormitory Life in Sweden   83

(5) My friend is so rich! He (　　　　　　　　) his house which has six bedrooms, five bathrooms and a huge garden.

## 2. *Grammar*
空所に適語を入れてそれぞれ2つの表現が同じような意味になるようにしなさい。

(1) A. Neither athletes nor students can keep improving their abilities if they do not try hard every day.

　　B. It is not possible for (　　) sports professionals or students to make progress if they do not make a serious effort daily.

　　① either　　　　② both　　　　③ not only　　　　④ whether

(2) A. I was able to install the software as the instructions were written not only in Swedish but also in English.

　　B. The software instructions were written in English as (　　) as in Swedish, making it possible for me to install it.

　　① much　　　　② many　　　　③ well　　　　④ good

## 3. *Understanding the Text*
次の質問に英語で答えなさい。

(1) What do Sweden and Japan have in common, according to the passage?
　　They both have an _____.

(2) Why did Yuto sleep deeply?
　　He did so because he was _____.

(3) What confused Yuto in the dormitory kitchen?
　　There were _____.

(4) What would Yuto like to do after graduating from university?
　　_____.

(5) Does Yuto have to learn the Swedish language? Why/Why not?
　　_____.

## IV. Listening

### 1. *Filling in the Blanks*

ユウトが、彼と同じ寮に住んでいるスウェーデン人学生のサラと話しています。CD を聴いて各空所に1語を入れなさい。

Track 52
Track 53

#### Yuto and Sara's Conversation

| Part 1 | 1. Sara is sure that Yuto is _____ many new things. |
| --- | --- |
| | 2. Yuto had a _____ about volunteer work. |
| | 3. Volunteer work is an important part of Swedish _____ lives. |
| Part 2 | 1. Sara asks Yuto to _____ them. |
| | 2. Yuto didn't know there was such a _____ in the university. |
| | 3. The club members often visit _____ schools. |

### 2. *Understanding the Dialog*

次は先ほどの会話の一部です。読んで、質問に答えなさい。

*************************************************************

**From PART 1:** Students and Volunteer Work

**Sara:** *It must be hard for you to get used to life in Sweden.*

**Yuto:** *Not at all! I'm learning so much every day.*

(1) Is Yuto having a hard time getting used to his life?

_____.

*************************************************************

**From PART 2:** Sara's Club

**Sara:** *In the summer, we travel abroad to the Philippines to work with children.*

**Yuto:** *Really? I have always wanted to visit other Asian countries. Please tell me how I can join.*

(2) What information does Yuto ask Sara for?

_____.

### Information Column: Fika in Sweden

スウェーデンには *fika*（フィーカ）と呼ばれる国民的習慣があります。休憩をとってコーヒーを飲み、友人や同僚と談笑します。日本では会社員があわただしくコーヒーを飲みほして仕事に戻っていく姿が見かけられますが、スウェーデンでは急ぎません。20 分近くゆっくりとした時間を過ごします。*fika* は少なくても午前 10 時と午後 3 時の 2 回は行います。*fika* をするときは、コーヒーのほかにたいていビスケットやケーキをいただきます。'Semla' というクリームがいっぱい挟んであるお菓子パンが有名です。スウェーデンでは多くの企業が社内に *fika* を楽しむスペースを設けて無料でコーヒーとケーキを提供しています。*fika* はスウェーデン人にとってなくてはならない憩いの機会なのです。

## V. Collocations

**1.** 語と語のつながりに注目して空所に最も適切な語を入れなさい。

(1) Yuto had a (　　　　　) **appetite** when he woke up. He ate three slices of toast, two bowls of cereal, three fried eggs and two apples.

　① big　　　　② hungry　　　③ small　　　　④ thirsty
　　R　　　　　　Y　　　　　　　Q　　　　　　　V

(2) Sweden has a (　　　　　) **population density**. Only nine million people live in a country larger than Japan.

　① few　　　　② many　　　　③ low　　　　　④ high
　　O　　　　　　T　　　　　　　S　　　　　　　E

(3) Yuto and his friends enjoy watching sports popular in Sweden. He has even become a (　　　　　) **fan** of the local ice hockey team.

　① extreme　　② huge　　　　③ stretched　　④ large
　　U　　　　　　A　　　　　　　I　　　　　　　E

(4) Sara thinks that participating in club activities is (　　　　　) **part of** university life. She always looks forward to the next club meeting.

　① an integral　② a separated　③ a joined　　④ a needed
　　H　　　　　　G　　　　　　　V　　　　　　　R

**2.** 各正解選択肢の下にある赤色ローマ字を組み合わせて空所に入る単語を作りなさい。

People who don't think carefully can tend to make (　　　　　) decisions.

## VI. Writing

下記はユウトのブログの一部です。日本語に合うように下記の英文の続きを、与えられた語句を組み合せて完成しなさい。ただし、それぞれ1語を補い、文頭は大文字に直しなさい。

> スウェーデンは日本人が英語を学ぶのにとてもよいところだと思います。ここの人々が話す英語は理解するのが容易です。(1) スウェーデン人は言葉を1つずつ丁寧に発音しますし、それほど速く話したりしません。(2) 英語の能力はここに来て以来、大きく改善しました。

I think Sweden is a great place for Japanese people to learn English. It is very easy to understand the English that people here speak.

(1)　① the Swedes pronounce　② each word carefully　③ do not speak　④ too quickly

_____.

(2)　① arriving here　② lot since　③ has improved a　④ my English

_____.

## VII. What Can You Do Now?

最後に下記の3つの到達目標を読んで、できるものにチェックを入れなさい。

*I can*

☐ *talk about the recycling system in Sweden.*

☐ *explain what the Swedish custom of 'fika' is.*

☐ *give reasons why Sweden is a good place for Japanese to learn English.*

# Chapter 14　Volunteer Work in the Philippines
フィリピンのボランティア活動（フィリピン）

本章ではスウェーデンの留学先で知り合ったユウトとサラが、フィリピンでボランティア活動をします。

## I. Vocabulary Preview

本章で扱う語(句)です。それぞれの意味を表す日本語を選びなさい。

1. archipelago　(　)　2. remote　(　)　3. equipment　(　)
4. impoverished　(　)　5. sewage systems　(　)　6. deserve　(　)

> a. 辺ぴな　　　　b. 貧困にあえいで　　c. 〜に値する
> d. 公共施設　　　e. 備品　　　　　　　f. 諸島
> g. 下水システム

## II. Introduction

本章で扱う内容の紹介です。英文にさっと目を通して、次の問いに英語で答えなさい。　Track 54

> 　　Yuto, a Japanese university student majoring in childhood studies, studied abroad at a Swedish university. There, he met Sara, a female Swedish student, and she invited him to join the volunteer club. Now, Yuto and Sara have gone with other club members to the Philippines, where they will help with a project called "Education Village." Let's find out what adventures they have.

(1) Will Yuto travel to the Philippines alone?

(2) What is the name of the project the volunteer club is working on? What do you think the project is about?

## III. Reading

サラとユウトの会話です。読んで問いに答えなさい。

Track 55

**Sara:** **I thought we'd never get here**! This island was difficult to get to. Furthermore, this village is so far from the nearest town.

**Yuto:** Yes, the Philippines is an archipelago nation, so some places are very isolated.

**Sara:** Yuto, what do you remember about our job?

**Yuto:** Well, the Education Village is an initiative created to improve the lives of people in poverty in remote areas of the Philippines. Our job is to continue the work of the volunteers who came here before us.

**Sara:** **You've hit the nail on the head.** To **expand on** what you said, first we have to talk with the volunteer group going home in a few days. They will tell us what they've done and what work is expected of us.

**Yuto:** I see. The buildings here look quite new. Are you sure this village is impoverished?

**Sara:** Local and foreign volunteer teams construct and continually maintain the buildings together, keeping them looking new. Similarly, they have also constructed sewage systems, drinking water pumps, **and the like**.

**Yuto:** I'm looking forward to our work, which includes helping to teach the local children about science and mathematics. I hope our supplies have arrived.

**Sara:** I heard that the supplies arrived yesterday. They include books, other educational equipment, and some standard items such as medicine and tools. Such supplies are purchased using money donated by governments and individuals all over the world.

**Yuto:** I was pleased to hear that some donations came from Japan and Sweden. This volunteer work deserves such **warm support**.

## 1. *Words & Phrases*

本文の太字の語句の中から適切なものを選んで空所に記入しなさい。

(1) A: Do you have any questions about the lecture?
   B: I didn't understand the final part. Could you (                    ) what you said, please?

(2) I'm glad to be home at last. We were stuck in a traffic jam for three hours.
   (                    )!

(3) A: Enthusiasm is very important if you want to really learn anything.
   B: (                    ). I completely agree with you.

(4) Our favorite charity is "Education for the Poor." We give it our (　　　　　　　　).

(5) My friend likes all types of Japanese food. In fact, she likes eating *sushi, tofu, miso soup,* (　　　　　　　　).

## 2. *Grammar*
空所に適語を入れてそれぞれ 2 つの表現が同じような意味になるようにしなさい。

(1) A. It was very comfortable on the sofa.
　　B. The sofa was very comfortable to (　　　　　).
　　① sit　　　　② sit on　　　　③ lay　　　　④ sit up

(2) A. The problem was difficult to solve.
　　B. I (　　　　　) it difficult to solve the problem.
　　① took　　　② regarded　　　③ found　　　④ cost

## 3. *Understanding the Text*
次の質問に英語で答えなさい。

(1) Why was the Education Village project created?
　　It was created to improve _____.

(2) What will the volunteer group that is leaving soon tell Yuto and Sara's group?
　　They will tell them what _____.

(3) Why do some buildings in the village look new?
　　They look new because _____.

(4) What does Sara and Yuto's work include?
　　_____.

(5) Aside from standard items such as medicine and tools, what supplies arrived yesterday?
　　_____.

# IV. Listening

## 1. Filling in the Blanks

Track 56
Track 57

ユウトが、他のボランティア講師のリタと話しています。CD を聴いて各空所に 1 語を入れなさい。

### Yuto and Rita's Conversation

| Part 1 | 1. Yuto did well, _____ it was his first day. |
| | 2. The children realize that _____ an education is wonderful. |
| | 3. In the past, the nearest school was a long _____ away. |
| Part 2 | 1. Yuto would like to _____ a lot more. |
| | 2. He would like to work _____ more in the Education Village. |
| | 3. Rita asks Yuto to come and give them a _____ repainting the school. |

## 2. Understanding the Dialog

次は先ほどの会話の一部です。読んで、質問に答えなさい。

*******************************************************************************

**From PART 1:** At the End of Yuto's First Day

**Rita:** *The children appreciated your work very much, Yuto.*

**Yuto:** *Thank you. I was surprised at how enthusiastic they all were.*

(1) What surprised Yuto?

_____.

*******************************************************************************

**From PART 2:** Always Work to Do

**Rita:** *You are staying with a local family, right? Why don't you offer to do some chores?*

**Yuto:** *That's a good idea.*

(2) What does Yuto think is a good idea?

_____.

### ✈ **Information Column: Volunteer Work**

　この章では登場人物のユウトが発展途上国のボランティアに出かけました。実際のところ、国内外の各地でボランティアの支援を必要としており、数多くの団体が参加者を募っています。近年では若者だけではなく、退職された方々の積極的な参加も目立つようになってきました。ボランティア活動は参加者にどのような変化をもたらすのでしょうか。海外のボランティア活動では、金銭面の負担のほか、その国の事情に応じて様々な苦労やときには危険が伴うことも当然想定されますが、ここではそのプラス面について次の5つの項目をあげます。

1. 純粋に他者の役に立つ
2. 単なる旅行者とは異なる観点から地域の人々のくらしを知る
3. 人間としての成長を促すきっかけになる
4. コミュニケーションスキルを向上させる
5. 同じような考えをもつ人々と仲間になる

## 🌐 V. Collocations

**1.** 語と語のつながりに注目して空所に最も適切な語を入れなさい。

(1) Volunteers are (　　　　) **workers**, meaning they do not get a salary for their work.

　① moneyless　　② private　　③ public　　④ unpaid
　　　A　　　　　　　　I　　　　　　　　U　　　　　　　　O

(2) Volunteers do not expect to stay in high-class hotels. They often stay in modest accommodation and (　　　　) **a room** with others.

　① divide　　② distribute　　③ share　　④ collaborate
　　　A　　　　　　　E　　　　　　　O　　　　　　　I

(3) Even office workers take a **career** (　　　　) to become a volunteer these days. They can then return to work after the program.

　① stop　　② pause　　③ break　　④ quit
　　　P　　　　　Z　　　　　R　　　　　K

(4) The people helped by volunteers always remember their (　　　　) **of kindness.**

　① play　　② act　　③ performance　　④ feat
　　　J　　　　F　　　　　V　　　　　B

**2.** 各正解選択肢の下にある赤色ローマ字を組み合わせて空所に入る単語を作りなさい。

　Yuto was lucky because a local family allowed him to live under the same (　　　　　　　) as them during his time as a volunteer.

92　Let's Get Out of Japan!

## VI. Writing

下記はユウトのブログの一部です。日本語に合うように下記の英文の続きを、与えられた語句を組み合せて完成しなさい。ただし、それぞれ1語を補い、文頭は大文字に直しなさい。

> ここの子供たちは学用品の数が少ないので教科書を共有して使っています。しかし、子供たちは熱意があり、物覚えがはやいです。(1) 学校で食事が提供されるので子供たちは授業中お腹がすきません。(2) このプログラムは子供たちの未来を切り開くために、教育の機会を提供します。

*The children here share textbooks as the supply is limited. However, they are enthusiastic and are quick learners.*

(1)　① the lessons　② meals are provided　③ at school so they　④ are not hungry

_____.

(2)　① this program　② to education　③ , improving their future　④ gives them

_____.

## VII. What Can You Do Now?

最後に下記の3つの到達目標を読んで、できるものにチェックを入れなさい。

*I can*

☐ *say something about the work done by a volunteer program in the Philippines.*

☐ *talk a little about the living conditions a volunteer can expect.*

☐ *list some benefits of volunteering abroad.*

# Chapter 15 *Around the World on a Volunteer Ship*
## 世界をめぐるボランティア活動（ボランティア船）

最終章では世界を回る船に乗って、各地でボランティア活動を行う学生が登場します。

## I. Vocabulary Preview

本章で扱う語（句）です。それぞれの意味を表す日本語を選びなさい。

1. persuade      (     )    2. mission       (     )    3. promote      (     )
4. demonstration (     )    5. disembark     (     )    6. on board     (     )

| | | |
|---|---|---|
| a. 促進する | b. 説得する | c. 船上で |
| d. 実演 | e. 使命 | f. 下船する |
| g. 扱う | | |

## II. Introduction

本章で扱う内容の紹介です。英文にさっと目を通して、次の問いに英語で答えなさい。

Track 58

　　Masafumi, a Japanese university student, heard about a ship called a Volunteer Ship. It is filled with volunteers of many nationalities and visits many countries to communicate with the local people there. The ship's mission is to promote understanding between different cultures. An exchange student at Masafumi's university, Linda, persuaded him to join her on the ship during their summer vacation. The ship will sail all around the world. Let's find out what adventures they have.

(1) What is the ship's mission?


(2) Why do you think Linda wanted Masafumi to join the Volunteer Ship with her?

## III. Reading

日本からの乗船を前にしてリンダとマサフミがボランティアの旅について話し合います。
読んで問いに答えなさい。

Track 59

**Linda:** We will leave Japan next week! I am so excited. **According to** the schedule, our first **port of call** is Busan, in the Republic of Korea.

**Masafumi:** **I can hardly wait**! I'm looking forward to speaking to the local people there. However, I don't speak Korean!

**Linda:** Have you read the list of volunteers? People from over 60 different countries will be on the ship, including from Korea, so I'm sure someone can translate for us. Anyway, we can communicate with each other speaking English.

**Masafumi:** I didn't read the list yet as I was busy preparing my presentation about Japan. We will visit schools in each country we stop at and talk to the children there about our countries. I'm going to read some Japanese folk tales and play the *taiko* drum. Let's **do a demonstration** of a *yosakoi* dance together, shall we? Doing that would be a good way to explain Japanese culture to people.

**Linda:** Great! After Korea, we'll be stopping at Thailand, India, Saudi Arabia and Turkey. Then, we'll visit some more countries before reaching our **final destination**, France.

**Masafumi:** Yes, the ship will continue on its voyage around the world but we have to disembark at France. We only have two months summer holidays so we'll have to get off to catch a plane home. **It's a pity** we can't stay on board for the whole trip.

**Linda:** Don't worry about that—let's just enjoy the two months we will have. I think we'll have a wonderful time both on land and at sea.

### 1. *Words & Phrases*

本文の太字の語句の中から適切なものを選んで空所に記入しなさい。

(1) It has been very cold this winter. (　　　　　　　　) for winter to finish and spring to begin.

(2) I think it is easier to understand what someone is talking about if they (　　　　　　　　).

(3) (　　　　　　　　) that Masafumi and Linda have to leave the ship in France. They wish their summer holiday was longer.

(4) Cruises often have different events planned at each (　　　　　　　　).

(5) The traveler visited places all over the world but, when he got old, his
(      ) was his country of birth.

## 2. *Grammar*

空所に適語を入れてそれぞれ 2 つの表現が同じような意味になるようにしなさい。

(1) A. Australia sent their national team to the Asian Football Championship, making a total of ten teams.
 B. Ten national teams, (  ) one from Australia, participated in the Asian Football Championship.
  ① sending    ② including    ③ departing    ④ appearing

(2) A. My father was always very quiet, though he responded if somebody spoke to him.
 B. My father was a very quiet person. He didn't speak unless (  ) to.
  ① speak    ② spoken    ③ spoke    ④ speaks

## 3. *Understanding the Text*

次の質問に英語で答えなさい。

(1) What is Masafumi looking forward to?
 He is looking forward to speaking _____.

(2) What did Linda learn by reading the list of volunteers?
 She learned that people _____.

(3) Why didn't Masafumi read the list?
 He was busy _____.

(4) What does Masafumi say the advantage of doing a *yosakoi* demonstation would be?
_____.

(5) How will Masafumi and Linda return to Japan from France?
_____.

## IV. Listening

### 1. *Filling in the Blanks*

マサフミが、韓国人ボランティアのジンさんとボランティア船の船上で話しています。彼らは今、韓国を出航したばかりでこれからタイに向かいます。CD を聴いて各空所に 1 語を入れなさい。

Track 60
Track 61

#### Masafumi and Jin's Conversation

| Part 1 | 1. Masafumi had a lot of _____ in Busan. |
| --- | --- |
|  | 2. His demonstrations were very _____ , making them easy for everyone. |
|  | 3. Masafumi wanted everyone to get his _____ . |
| Part 2 | 1. Their next _____ will be at Thailand. |
|  | 2. Jin is looking forward to doing a _____ there. |
|  | 3. Masafumi thinks that Jin's presentation will be full of interesting _____ . |

### 2. *Understanding the Dialog*

次は先ほどの会話の一部です。読んで、質問に答えなさい。

*************************************************************************

**From PART 1:** A Successful Presentation

**Jin:** *The children at the school we visited in Busan loved your presentation about Japan.*

**Masafumi:** *It's amazing that they could understand English so well.*

(1) What did Masafumi find amazing?

_____.

*************************************************************************

**From PART 2:** So Much to Learn

**Jin:** *I thought you learned a lot while we were there.*

**Masafumi:** *This Volunteer Ship has given me the chance to experience so many new cultures —I want to take full advantage of it.*

(2) What does Masafumi want to take advantage of?

_____.

*Chapter 15 Around the World on a Volunteer Ship* **97**

### Information Column: Volunteer Ships

様々なタイプのボランティア船が異なる使命を持って世界の海を航海しています。異なる文化間の理解を促進することを目的とする船もあれば、紛争地域を訪れて医療品や食糧を提供して世界の平和を考えることを目的とする船もあります。ボランティアたちは、停泊後各地で現地の人との交流をすすめるために多彩な催しものを企画運営します。船上では次の催し物の準備をし、船内の維持管理にもできる範囲で協力します。各種の工学技術や料理の技を持っていれば、別な形でボランティア船の運航に貢献する人もいます。参加者は原則、自分たちの食費や船舶での滞在費を負担しながら、他ではなかなか経験できない体験を積んでいきます。

## V. Collocations

1. 語と語のつながりに注目して空所に最も適切な語を入れなさい。

(1) While at sea, Masafumi was assigned to the cooking team. However, as he hated cooking, he **applied** (　　　) a transfer to the cleaning team instead.
① for　　　② at　　　③ on　　　④ near
　T　　　　　H　　　　P　　　　C

(2) Linda thought she was **incapable** (　　　) living for two months without an internet connection, but she got used to it quickly.
① by　　　② of　　　③ up　　　④ in
　E　　　　　I　　　　A　　　　I

(3) Masafumi and Linda **embarked** (　　　) a journey they would remember for their whole lives.
① at　　　② in　　　③ on　　　④ by
　A　　　　　E　　　　H　　　　U

(4) Linda **suffered** (　　　) sea sickness during the first day at sea, but she recovered and felt much better.
① about　　② from　　③ upon　　④ over
　G　　　　　W　　　　B　　　　R

2. 各正解選択肢の下にある赤色ローマ字を組み合わせて空所に入る単語を作りなさい。

Masafumi and Linda made many friends on the ship. They were sad when they had to part (　　　) them in France.

98　Let's Get Out of Japan!

## VI. Writing

下記はマサフミのブログの一部です。日本語に合うように下記の英文の続きを、与えられた語句を組み合わせて完成しなさい。ただし、それぞれ1語を補い、文頭は大文字に直しなさい。

> 私たちの航海は今や6週間を過ぎました。船上の私たちはみな1つの大きな家族のようです。(1) 明日はトルコ、3日後にはイタリアを訪れます。(2) この船のボランティアとして、毎日感じている喜びを表現するのはむずかしいです。

**Our voyage has lasted a little over six weeks now. All of us on board feel like one big family.**

(1)  ① visit Turkey, followed   ② by Italy   ③ three days   ④ tomorrow, we will

_____.

(2)  ① the joy I feel   ② it is difficult to   ③ volunteer on this ship   ④ everyday as a

_____.

## VII. What Can You Do Now?

最後に下記の3つの到達目標を読んで、できるものにチェックを入れなさい。

*I can*

☐ give examples of some things a Japanese person could demonstrate to people of other cultures.

☐ describe different types of "volunteer ships."

☐ say what can be gained by working on a volunteer ship.

# Review Test III
## Chapters 12-15

*Choose the most suitable word or phrase for each blank space.*

1. My grandfather is interested in European culture. He has a …… collection of German, French and Dutch artefacts.
    - A. competitive
    - B. strict
    - C. well
    - D. fine

2. International trade is a …… part of Japan's economy.
    - A. needed
    - B. vital
    - C. nauseous
    - D. vicious

3. Losing the match made the team even more …… improve their skills.
    - A. determined to
    - B. determined for
    - C. determined of
    - D. determined with

4. Scientists …… their knowledge by carrying out experiments and reading other people's research.
    - A. excavate
    - B. deepen
    - C. hollow out
    - D. scoop in

5. The course greatly …… my expectations. I hadn't thought I'd learn so much in such a short time.
    - A. expanded
    - B. outreached
    - C. overcame
    - D. exceeded

6. On his first day, the new employee …… a good start by arriving early and introducing himself.
    - A. made
    - B. did
    - C. was
    - D. talked

7. Scholarships can help students to …… their dream of getting a university degree.
    - A. realize
    - B. adjust
    - C. open
    - D. supervise

8. One …… some companies fail is that they lack innovative ideas.
    - A. case that
    - B. reason why
    - C. way how
    - D. fact that

9. Finishing the marathon left me …… exhausted yet also gave me a feeling of satisfaction.
    - A. sporadically
    - B. quickly
    - C. completely
    - D. culturally

10. The government still hasn't …… a solution to the aging population in Japan.
    - A. developed for
    - B. shaped up
    - C. pointed in
    - D. figured out

11. Every spring, thousands of salmon …… up rivers in Hokkaido to lay their eggs.
    - A. make their way
    - B. go their path
    - C. do their road
    - D. have their lot

12. On our …… at the restaurant, we noticed that all the tables were full.
    - A. arrival
    - B. waiting
    - C. meal
    - D. reservation

**13.** A company can increase profits by being careful not to …… resources.
   A. waste    B. use    C. spend    D. throw

**14.** A small …… of kindness can make a big impact on someone's life.
   A. performance    B. act    C. drama    D. function

**15.** Diamonds, rubies, emeralds, and …… like can be used in making expensive jewelry.
   A. a    B. the    C. one    D. those

**16.** My seven-year-old son is 140cm tall. That is quite tall, …… his age.
   A. stretching    B. counting    C. registering    D. considering

**17.** A friend is a person who gives you a …… when you are in trouble.
   A. leg    B. arm    C. hand    D. foot

**18.** The old man hit the …… on the head when he said that education is useless without enthusiasm.
   A. nail    B. stick    C. statue    D. nuance

**19.** Knowing she had the …… support of her family gave the girl more confidence.
   A. cold    B. cool    C. warm    D. hot

**20.** The employee was …… to the international sales division because of her strong English skills.
   A. assigned    B. employed    C. established    D. aligned

**21.** I didn't understand what she was trying to tell me, but it became clear when she …… a demonstration.
   A. created    B. did    C. had    D. saw

**22.** I had a great time speaking to you at the party. I can …… until we meet again!
   A. softly play    B. hardly wait    C. severely talk    D. rapidly dance

**23.** It's …… the athlete became ill before the competition. I was sure he was going to win.
   A. a pity    B. the shame    C. a nationality    D. the problem

**24.** The mother was heartbroken when she had to …… her son who got a job in another country.
   A. part of    B. part with    C. part to    D. part in

**25.** People who don't eat healthily tend to suffer …… illness more than those who do.
   A. over    B. in    C. from    D. to

# Phrase List

## Chapter 1
change so much
confidence in
enroll in
exchange emails
gain knowledge

in addition to
look (something) up
make progress
miss (a bus, etc)
pack a suitcase

pay attention to
pick (somebody) up
save money
scenic beauty
spend money

stand to attention
waste money
work part time

## Chapter 2
achieve goals
bungee jumping
come across
common expressions
concentrate on
dairy products

deep breath
enjoy every moment
get by
go downtown
heavy sleeper
(be) involved in

light sleeper
locally-produced
manage to
regular exercise
(an alarm) rings
spend time

strong coffee
take a bath
take a breath
take care of (one's) health
time passes
treat (someone) as

## Chapter 3
afternoon tea
come to a conclusion
consider doing
due to
economic conditions
encourage (someone) to

get a job
(a) lively accent
local area
lost and found
lunch break
make a difference

popular destination
rented apartment
sense of humour
social situations
take care of
that is not the case

the other day
to major in (something)
to wonder if/whether

## Chapter 4
a second opinion
an approach to
as you know
business-oriented
chewing gum
completely trust
daily life
disadvantage

equal and fair
ethnic background
fresh breath
geographical area
hold an event
(an) ideal way to
immigrate to
make (oneself) understood

melting pot
multi-ethnic society
natural resources
one in three
opportunity of doing
public relations
safety and comfort
serve (a meal)

take advantage of
thriving economy
valuable experience
working conditions
working holiday

## Chapter 5
allergic to
arrivals gate
brown bread
carry-on luggage
Central Europe

check-in luggage
connecting flight
conveyor belt
direct flight
European Union

first taste of
have a shower
perceive things
point of view
put trust in

rich history
speak a language
tell stories
turn off the television
with a hug

## Chapter 6
apply for
arrange (things) neatly
college graduate
develop an interest
domestic and international
food and shelter
free time

gap between (A and B)
home and abroad
in need of
language barrier
let a problem slide
NGO (non-governmental organization)

occupied by
part-time job
poorly paid
social welfare
solve a problem
take up a job offer
think for yourself

treat (someone) with respect
use (one's) initiative
welfare system
well-paid

## Chapter 7
allow (someone) to
be fed up with
depend on
detailed information

hard (to do)
high score
language institute
(one's) own

placement test
recommend (someone) to
seek help from
spend time doing

take advice
travel abroad

## Chapter 8
appealing to
commit a crime
distance education
drop of rain
early settler
envy (someone)

flora and fauna
from scratch
geographic isolation
inspire (someone) to
petty crimes
precious resource

raise (one's) young
rural areas
struggle to
tell a joke
tube of toothpaste
unique to

untouched by
vast land
without pay
work overtime

*Let's Get Out of Japan!*

## Chapter 9

and so forth
avoid doing
double-decker bus
enable (someone) to
get on well with
get used to

ginger hair
in advance
in common
miss a flight
open-top bus
overcome a problem

persuade (someone) to
practical advice
private life
put an idea in (one's) mind
red hair
repair work

return ticket
student discount
suit (someone)
to be honest
transfer (someone) to
(dormitory) unit

## Chapter 10

academic achievement
adapt to (a situation)
be/become skilled in
break the law
business and pleasure
completely different matter

construction worker
develop (one's) personality
fluent in
give advice
housemaid
issue a visa

job seeker
keep a diary
make a presentation
make a profit
piece of advice
send by post

skills and qualifications
work abroad
work ethic

## Chapter 11

a little outside
a small population
appealing point
be born and raised
benefit of
convert into
find a job

from generation to generation
go around (a city, etc.)
hand down
have a headache
historic site
hot spot
improve (one's) skills

in this vicinity
large number of
local ingredients
make (one's) bed
natural scenery
off the coast
reasonable price

spacious countryside
speaking skills
take (someone) on a trip
tourism industry
tourist destination
try on (clothes)
unique customs

## Chapter 12

a fine collection of
a unique way
a vital part of
a wide range of knowledge
anything from (A) to (B)
application form
attend an interview
be determined to

be nervous at (an event)
be out of work
benefit from
conduct an interview
deal with customers
deepen (one's) knowledge
enable (one) to
experience of (doing)

find a balance
get accepted to
give a perspective on/of
greatly exceed
internship program
job satisfaction
light up (a building, etc.)
live abroad

make a good impression
make a good start
on the other hand
pass over
prepare well
provided (that)
realize (one's) dream of (doing)
staff member

## Chapter 13

a custom of
a low/high population density
a positive attitude
a reason why
an integral part of
childhood studies
communicate in (a language)

completely exhausted
culture shock
disturb nature
dormitory life
figure out
get on well
have a hard time

have (something) in common
make (one's) way
native language
on (one's) arrival
participate in
recycling system
shared kitchen

show (someone) around
transport system
university major
volunteer work
waste resources

## Chapter 14

act of kindness
an initiative
and the like
archipelago nation
career break
drinking water

educational equipment
expand on
get an education
give (someone) a hand
high-class hotel
hit the nail on the head

I thought we'd never get here
live under the same roof
modest accommodation
people of working age
quick learner
remote area

sewage system
standard items
stuck in a traffic jam
unpaid workers
warm support

## Chapter 15

a good way to
according to
be assigned to
capable of (doing)
(one's) country of birth
do a demonstration

embark on
exchange student
final destination
folk tales
followed by
I can hardly wait

it's a pity
not speak unless spoken to
on board
part with (someone)
participate in
port of call

promote understanding
sea sickness
suffer from

| 著作権法上，無断複写・複製は禁じられています。|

## Let's Get Out of Japan! [B-787]

英語で世界に橋を架けよう ～海外で学ぶ・働く・異文化を知るための総合英語～

| 第1刷 | 2015年3月20日 |
| 第4刷 | 2023年6月8日 |

| 著 者 | 川村　義治　　Yoshiharu Kawamura |
| | リンチ・ギャビン　　Gavin Lynch |

| 発行者 | 南雲一範　Kazunori Nagumo |
| 発行所 | 株式会社　南雲堂 |
| | 〒162-0801　東京都新宿区山吹町361 |
| | NAN'UN-DO Publishing Co., Ltd. |
| | 361 Yamabuki-cho, Shinjuku-ku, Tokyo 162-0801, Japan |
| | 振替口座：00160-0-46863 |
| | TEL：03-3268-2311（営業部：学校関係） |
| | 　　　03-3268-2384（営業部：書店関係） |
| | 　　　03-3268-2387（編集部） |
| | FAX：03-3269-2486 |

| 編集者 | 丸小　雅臣 |
| 表　紙 | 奥定　泰之 |
| 組版・印刷 | 啓文堂 |
| 検　印　省　略 |
| コード | ISBN978-4-523-17787-6 C0082 |

Printed in Japan

落丁・乱丁，その他不良品がございましたら，お取り替えいたします。

E-mail　nanundo@post.email.ne.jp
URL　https://www.nanun-do.co.jp/